PAUL VERHOEVEN
Beyond Flesh and Blood

Foreword by
Ed Neumeier

I suppose that my films are so controversial simply because I do what an artist is supposed to do — raise many emotional and violent reactions.

Paul Verhoeven

Jean-Marc Bouineau
[Supervision: Gilles Boulenger]

Le Cinéphage

Front cover:
Paul Verhoeven on *Hollow Man* (© Stephen Vaughan/SMPSP)
Back cover:
Quotation from Peter Weller (© *Paul Verhoeven*, Faber & Faber)

First published in France in 1994
by SpartOrange

First published in Great Britain in 2001
by Cinéditions
66 Champs Elysées 75008 Paris - France

Lay-out: Eric Martin, Lydie Durand
Printed in France by Augustin S.A.

A CIP record for this book
is available from the British Library

ISBN 2-9516306-0-3

"Everyone fights, no one quits!"

(Rasczak in Starship Troopers)

We are driving to the set for the first day of principal photography. The movie we are making is an enormous undertaking, easily the largest and most ambitious movie any of us have ever been involved with. Between the producers and the director there is ninety years of practical filmmaking experience and at least ten hit movies, which are still watched today. The technical teams, swelling to more than 100, are veterans of many productions. They have worked for directors like David Lean, James Cameron and Steven Spielberg. Many have Academy Award statuettes at home as proof of their technical wizardry.

Afterwards you ask yourself, "How much better does it get?" but that's not how it felt that morning as we headed off for the first of 122 days of production on *Starship Troopers*. There was an awful feeling of dread hanging in the air. The director, Paul Verhoeven, was in a shitty mood, and neither his plucky associate producer, Stacey Lumbrezer, nor I were particularly motivated to talk to him when he was like this. I could only imagine Paul's state of mind this morning, something like: What's there to say anyway? All that's left to do is shoot the movie, which will be hard and awful and unpleasant.

The drive from the Casper Wyoming Hilton to the appropriately named 'Hell's Half Acre State Park' we were using to double as an alien landscape for our science fiction epic was far too long to endure in silence, so presently Ms. Lumbrezer and I are chatting away about nothing in particular. It reminds me of the way I joked with the Ob/GYN between labor pains when my wife was giving birth to our son.

When we arrive at the set, there are already several hundred people at work. It looks like a small village or, given the subject of our movie, a military encampment. Ms Lumbrezer — who at the time was trying to finish her first screenplay — exclaimed, "Well, Ed, now you've done it!" meaning I had written a script that was being filmed, "and now you know how it's done!" meaning it was all green lights and premieres from here on out, I suppose. She was, perhaps, too young to remember I had written *RoboCop* for Paul ten years earlier. I could hardly blame her. It seemed like a long time ago to me too, so I replied, half in jest, "Yes, but by the time we're done, I'll have forgotten how I did it."

And then, to my great surprise, Mr. Verhoeven emerged briefly from the pit of distinctly Dutch despair he's brewed up for himself that morning and sadly announced, "Yes, that's the way it always is."

For me, a young man of relative inexperience, this was quite a revelation. Could it be that Paul Verhoeven, veteran director and world class bad boy, suffered from the same doubt and insecurity I did? It seemed nearly impossible at the time, but later Paul would tell me he was simply terrified. *Starship Troopers* was the hardest thing he'd ever done as a director, and because of the special effects schedule he was beginning with the most difficult sequence in the movie. I was wrong about one thing though. Paul didn't suffer from doubt and insecurity the way I did. He suffered much more. I guess that's why he was in such a bad mood that morning.

Ed Neumeier and Paul Verhoeven.

Now, as you read on about his views on violence, religion and ambiguity, keep in mind that I have already told you his greatest secret, perhaps the great secret recipe of all artistic endeavors. One should be terrified. It's not something you can fake, and maybe like class you're either born with it or you're not. But whatever the case, it's what makes Paul tick, I think, and why his movies, whether I am lucky enough to write them or not, are always fresh, vivid, and bracing.

Ed Neumeier
Eagle Rock, California
January 2001

1938. July 18th. Birth of Paul Verhoeven in Amsterdam.

1946-1949. Studies in the same school his father is teaching.

1949-1954. Enters the Gymnasium, the top level of secondary education in Holland.

1955. Sent to France by his parents. Attends L'Ecole de la Tour where he indulges his love for drawing. Learn how to speak french. Discovers the works of Jean Vigo, Henri-Georges Clouzot and Jean Renoir.

1956. Back in Holland, he enters Leiden University, the most prestigious university of the country. There he studies mathematics and physics for five years. Gets his first camera.

1959. Attends the newly founded Nederlandse FilmAcademie in Amsterdam but doesn't fit in. October. Directs *One Lizard too many*, a 35-minute short film about a disfunctionning couple. Budget: $1,000.

1960. June 15th. Première of *One Lizard too many* in the presence of Crown Princess Beatrix. The Leiden Academic Art Centre exposes *La Femme assise*, a painting Verhoeven made when he was planning to become a painter. It describes a blond naked woman seen from behind sitting on a rock and looking at a desolate landscape.

1962. Directs *The Hitchhikers* and *Nothing Special*. *The Hitchhikers* tells the story of three boys competing for a girl. *Nothing Special* is based on a quotation by William Faulkner.

1963. Spring. Shoots its fourth short film. Based on *Anton Wachter*, Simon Vestdijk's famous novel series, *Let's Have a Party* tells the story of the growing love between the 15 year old Anton Wachter and a girl in the second year. Budget: $8,500. Meets with his future wife, Martine Tours, a violin player.

1964. June. Gets his PhD in mathematics and physics. July. Drafted to The Hague Verhoeven is promoted lieutenant commander, assigned to the Marine Film Service and commissioned a 23-minute movie celebrating the tercentenary of the Dutch Marine Corps. Budget: $45,000.

1965. Autumn. Première of *The Marine Corps* in Rotterdam.

1966. Spring. After completing his two-year time in the military Verhoeven pens with the young novelist Kees Holierhoek a second chapter of Anton Wachter's life, Simon Vestdijk's novel series. But the producers are unable to secure financing for the movie.

1967. Tries to convince novelist Jan Wolkers to let him direct *Serpentina's Petticoat*, a recollection of Wolkers' World War II memories.

1968. Unable to get his big screen projects off the ground Verhoeven decides to shoot a documentary about Mussert, the leader of the NSB — a Dutch pro-fascist party created in the 30's. July 15th. The shooting of *Floris* — a Dutch *Ivanhoe* — starts. Made for the Dutch Television Foundation *Floris* is soon over-schedule and over-budget. The completion of the 12-episode series takes 8 months instead of the initially scheduled 14 weeks. The budget arises from $160,000 to $560,000. October 23rd. The broadcasting of *Portrait of Anton Adriaan Mussert* is cancelled at the last minute.

1969. October 5th. Airing of the first episode of *Floris*. In spite of its costly adjustments *Floris* is a huge success. Scripts with Soeteman a 6-part TV drama — each episode has the same starting point: a painting from Rembrandt.

1970. Writes with Soeteman *The Lansquenets* — the first draft of *Flesh + Blood*, a script inspired by Jan van Leyden's life, a charismatic leader who took over the town of Munster in 1542 and wanted to set there the New Jerusalem. Plans to direct a movie about Hans Van Z., a 26 year old necrophile, and Ouwe Nol, a first rate crook — the deadly duo had killed three people in 1969 with a lead pipe. Directs *The Wrestler*, a 20-minute burlesque scripted by Kees Holierhoek and photographed by newcomer Jan de Bont — the future director of *Twister* and Verhoeven's cinematographer on *The Fourth Man* and *Flesh + Blood*. Options Jan Wolkers' best seller *Turkish Delight*, but the project falls apart — Wolkers is indeed unable to meet the deadline for the treatment. April 16th. Broadcasting with minor changes of *Portrait of Anton Adriaan Mussert*. Is contacted by Rob Houwer, a shrewd businessman, to direct Albert Mol's *What's that I see? ... Conversations with Blonde Greet* — later to become *Business is Business* — a best seller published in 1965 compiling the twisted practices of the red light district clientele in Amsterdam. August. On the basis of the forty-page outline handed by Verhoeven Houwer grants him $280,000 to make the movie.

1971. September 10th. Première of *Business is Business*. To the astonishment of Verhoeven the film is a huge success. Final attendance: 2.36 million people. Autumn. Houwer buys for 16,000$ the rights for *Turkish Delight*.

1972. July 11. The shooting of *Turkish Delight* starts. Budget: $470,000.

1973. February 22nd. Première of *Turkish Delight*. The movie becomes the top grossing Dutch movie ever with 3.34 million admissions — and still is. Tries to convince Rob Houwer to produce Louis Couperus' *The Mountain of Light*, the story of a young homosexual priest who becomes Emperor during the decadent days of the Roman Empire. But Houwer finds the project too expensive and convinces Verhoeven to direct Neel Doff's *Keetje Tippel*, a grim tale with epic scale about a young prostitute who climbs the social ladder. Receives from French producer Pierre Braunberger a screenplay adapted from J.G. Ballard's *Crash*. Verhoeven: "Braunberger wanted me to do it — but I didn't... It was too dark."

1974. March. *Turkish Delight* is nominated for the Oscar of Best Foreign Film. April. Houwer rejects *Keetje Tippel's* 500-page script and menaces to close down the production. July. The 11-week shooting of *Keetje Tippel* starts. Budget: $930,000, the highest ever for a Dutch film.

1975. March 6. Première of *Keetje Tippel*. Attendance: 1.83 million people.

1976. September 25th. The 12-week shooting of *Soldier of Orange*, the adaptation of the memoirs of the freedom fighter Eric Hazelhoff Roelfzema, starts. Initial budget: $1.6 million. November 15th. The shooting is interrupted — Houwer needs additional money to finish the movie.

1977. Rank Organisation and the Dutch channel TROS inject an extra $700,000 to complete *Soldier of Orange*. April 17th. Verhoeven is given 5 five weeks to finish the movie. September 23rd. Première of *Soldier of Orange*. Attendance: 1.5 million people.

1978. With producer Joop van den Ende and Gerard Soeteman creates VSE Film, a production unit capable of delivering movies but also fictions for TV. First project: *Gone, Gone*. Pens with Gerard Soeteman the hyper-realistic *Spetters*. The Dutch Production Fund refuses to finance this "modern realistic Dutch drama" as Verhoeven sums it.

1979. Submits a revised draft of *Spetters* to The Dutch Production Fund, who this time accepts to finance the movie — Verhoeven decides nevertheless to shoot the original draft. August. Shooting of *Spetters* starts. Budget: $1.3 million. The US première of *Soldier of Orange* is a triumph.

1980. February. *Soldier of Orange* wins the Golden Globe for Best Foreign Movie. Première of *Spetters*. Vilified by the Dutch press the movie becomes the centre of a violent ostracism. Verhoeven decides to appear on a famous Dutch TV talk show to defend himself but the move is a disaster: homosexual militants try to kiss him in front of the camera and protests are coming from the audience, mainly disabled people. The same week an action group called The Dutch Anti-Spetters Action, supported by gays, women against pornography and the Pacifist Socialist Party, is created. Final attendance: 1.12 million people. Spring. Makes his first trip to Hollywood on the invitation of Steven Spielberg. With a bunch of scripts written by Soeteman Verhoeven meets with every studio executive in town. Warner Bros. is handed an adaptation of H.P. Lovecraft's *The Thing on the Doorstep* where a presidential adviser slowly looses it and starts to believe in the Armageddon. MGM is proposed *Harry's Tale*, a study of the slave trade in Africa during the 18th century. But even though all show interest the only studio who really wants to sign up Verhoeven is Columbia Pictures. Frank Price, then head of the studio, asks Verhoeven to consider directing *Death Comes as the End*, an Agatha Christie novel adapted by Anthony Shaffer. Budgeted at $10 million, set in Egypt and rewritten by Soeteman the movie is discarded when Price exits Columbia Pictures for Universal.

1981. June. Begins writing with Soeteman *The Fourth Man*, an adaptation of Gerard Reve's haunting thriller. A contention between Jeroen Krabbé, the actor Verhoeven wants for the lead, and Joop van den Ende, who bought the rights of the novel, stalls the whole project. Eager to make this movie and none other Verhoeven re-teams with Rob Houwer and buys the rights from Reve the minute Joop van den Ende's option has expired. VSE Film is dissolved.

1982. March. Rehearsals for *The Fourth Man* begin — shooting is being scheduled for May. Budget: $1.15 million.

1983. March 24th. Première of *The Fourth Man*. Attendance: 400,000 people. October 21st. Orion agrees to finance *God's own Butchers* — later to be renamed *Flesh + Blood*. The original outline written in 1980 was centring on the relationship between Martin and Hawkwood, two mercenaries who were buddies, chose different paths but meet again when Martin kidnaps Agnes, the bride of Hawkwood's boss' son, Steven. Though willing to pay out $7.5 million to finance *Flesh + Blood* Orion imposes that the Agnes-Steven love story be pushed to the foreground and that Nastassja Kinski or Rebecca de Mornay plays Agnes. Verhoeven complies with the script changes but picks for Agnès Jennifer Jason Leigh — who impressed him in *Fast Times at Ridgemont High*.

1984. March. The 14 week shooting of *Flesh + Blood* starts in Spain. Chaos rules from day one. The Spanish crew works as little as possible and the American actors just want to party. To avoid delays caused by awful weather conditions and Rutger Hauer unwillingness to follow his vision, Verhoeven decides to line up for each set-up three cameras.

1985. August 30th. Première of *Flesh + Blood* at the Venice Film Festival. September. Championed by Mike Medavoy, then head of Orion, Verhoeven leaves for the USA to work on *RoboCop*. Budget: $13 million. *Flesh + Blood* bombs at the US box office. October. Shoots in 7 days *The Last Scene*, a 25-minute episode for the HBO series, *The Hitchhiker*. Verhoeven: "That was my first experience in the States. The story of Alex appealed to me, but the main reason I did it was because I wanted to test whether I was able or not to direct an American crew..."

1986. June. The 14-week shooting of *RoboCop* starts but the $600,000 armor suit designed by Rob Bottin is still not ready. After two weeks in the shooting Peter Weller has finally the opportunity to try it... And it's a disaster. The method actor flips out and refuses to carry on with the movie. "I look like Gort in *The Day the Earth stood still!*" he bolts. Weller gets the firing treatment from Jon Davison, the producer, but agents and lawyers smooth things over.

1987. July 17th. Première of *RoboCop*. Though a success with its $53.4 million earned at the US box-office [$120 million worldwide], *RoboCop* is largely misinterpreted. For Ed Neumeier indeed, *RoboCop*'s screenwriter, the movie was intended to be a satire of Reaganics. But for the audience the "sad metal creature", as Peter Weller calls it, is seen as a pop icon, the avenger they were looking for.

1988. Works on a black comedy called *White Trash*. Intends to do a movie about the Spanish conquistador Cortez to be produced by Ed Pressman. Gets deeply involved in *Black Rain* with Michael Douglas — later to be directed by Ridley Scott — until he reads the 45 versions of *Total Recall*'s script.

1989. Polishes the second and third act of *Total Recall*. Written in 1979 by Dan O'Bannon and Ronald Shusett, *Total Recall* is an adaptation of Philip K. Dick's short story, *We can remember it for you wholesale*. For a long time the project seemed stuck in development hell. Walt Disney got involved for two years but no satisfying scripts sweated from the multiple drafts. Then Dino De Laurentiis bought out the rights and for seven years had several directors including Russell Mulcahy and David Cronenberg attached to the project. He was even on the verge of producing the doomed script in the spring of 1988 — $6 million had been invested in sets, Patrick Swayze had agreed to play Quaid and Bruce Beresford was at the helm. But De Laurentis had to pull the plug two weeks before production because he went bankrupt. Shusett thought then that his script was history until Arnold Schwarzenegger, who for a long time had his eyes on the project, convinced Carolco Pictures to buy back the rights from De Laurentiis and secure Verhoeven in the director's seat. April. The 20-week shooting of *Total Recall* starts in Mexico. Initial budget: $55 million. With a crew of 300, ceaseless fighting with the producer, eight sets to watch out, bad food and time-consuming shots Verhoeven exhausts himself to such an extent than during an outdoor night shoot he nearly passes out. Final budget: $65 million.

1990. June 1st. Première of *Total Recall*. US box-office: $120 million [worldwide box-office: $263 million]. Starts working on *Basic Instinct*. Budget: $45 million. Further to a very heated meeting with Verhoeven, screenwriter Joe Eszterhas — who got paid $3 million for the script — and producer Irwin Winkler pull out. Verhoeven asks Gary Goldman, who tightened the loose ends of the *Total Recall* script, to adjust *Basic Instinct*'s screenplay to his demands. Winkler is replaced by Alan Marshall [Verhoeven's faithful associate/producer since then]. Works with Polly Platt on Charles Bukowski's *Women*. Plans to do a movie about the siege of Leningrad. Verhoeven: "It's a very ambitious movie. I found that it is very hard to get an American screenwriter interested in this project, probably because identification with the people from Leningrad — who are all Russians — is difficult for an American."

1991. February. Sends the new *Basic Instinct* script to Eszterhas. The changes are so minor that Eszterhas buries the hatchet. April. The Gay and Lesbian Alliance Against Defamation [GLAAD] organizes a protest near the set of *Basic Instinct* — they assert that the screenplay is homophobic. A peace conference is organized: Verhoeven, Joe Eszterhas and Alan Marshall as well as four activist groups attend it. Although Verhoeven thinks the activists' demands are nonsensical Eszterhas sees things differently and decides to modify his script. Five days later, Verhoeven receives the revised script and goes berserk. Eszterhas and Verhoeven part again. Eager to defend his freedom of speech Verhoeven obtains from the San Francisco Superior Court a ruling restricting the near access of the set to the activists. July. End of the shooting of *Basic Instinct*. Starts tooling a screenplay for *Christ the Man*, his project on the real life and times of Jesus Christ — the project is still in development at Brooksfilms and Tri-Star.

1992. March 20th. Première of *Basic Instinct*. US box-office: $118 million [worldwide box-office: $353 million].

1993. Works on *Crusade* with Walon Green, a $120 million epic starring Arnold Schwarzenegger. The story: Hagen, a slave condemned to death in 1095, bails himself out by joining the First Crusade led by Godfrey of Bouillon. But gradually Hagen begins to doubt that freeing Jerusalem from the hands of the Muslims is really the goal of the "holy mission". Develops *Mistress of the Seas*, an explicit pirate saga with Geena Davis in the lead role.

1994. Because of *Mistress of the Seas*' $75 million pricetag Columbia wants an equal male lead to guarantee a box-office hit. Harrison Ford is mentioned. But Verhoeven doesn't want to compromise the story of Privateer Ann Bonney nor his artistic freedom. End of story. Summer. Carolco pulls the plug on *Crusade* though the 22,000 costumes have been tailored and contracts have been signed. Verhoeven: "It became a really good script. It was very provocative and offensive. I always wanted to do a movie about the Crusades. *Ivan the Terrible* would have been one of the main influences for the movie. I would have used Eisenstein style and set-ups, differently of course." November. The shooting of *Showgirls* starts in Las Vegas. Budget: $38 million. To retain total creative control and be authorized to deliver a NC-17 movie Verhoeven hands back 70% of his $6 million fee.

1995. Polishes with Ed Neumeier *Starship Troopers*' script. Adapted from Robert Heinlein's eponymous novel written in 1959 Verhoeven had been working on this 'giant bugs versus mankind in outer space' screenplay since 1993. September 22nd. Première of *Showgirls*. US box-office: $20 million [worldwide box-office: $37.7 million].

1996. May. The 18-week shooting of *Starship Troopers* starts. Budget: $100 million, 40 of which are dedicated to the sole special effects.

1997. Toys with the idea of a movie about Hitler. November 7th. Première of *Starship Troopers*. US box-office: $55 million [worldwide box-office: $121 million].

1998. Gets really involved in *Houdini*, a script about the famous magician. Verhoeven: "I worked on it for eight months. I abandoned it because I couldn't solve it. Now I know how to solve it but the project is in the hands of Ang Lee."

1999. Embarks on *Hollow Man*, a re-work of the invisible man myth. Verhoeven: "It is close to H.G. Wells' spirit but not to the original story. It would have been illegal to use it." September. The shooting of *Hollow Man* starts.

2000. August 4th. Première of *Hollow Man*. US box-office: $73 million [worldwide box-office: $190 million]. Projects: *Rasputin*; an adaptation of Guy de Maupassant's *Mont-Oriol* [See page 65 for more]; a movie about American soldiers searching for war criminals in Berlin in 1945/46 to be produced by Mike Medavoy. Virtual plans. Verhoeven: "I would like to do a sequel to *Starship Troopers*. Alan Marshall has talked recently to Sony about it. I always thought this story was not finished because there was more to tell and more to explore and more to show."

"You won't learn anything I don't want you to know."

(Catherine Tramell in Basic Instinct)

"I can feel them but I can't remember them"

(Murphy/RoboCop in RoboCop)

You experienced the world's cruelty when very young...

P.V.: When I was five or six, I lived in The Hague, and the war was raging all over. The Germans occupied Holland and the English, who tried to destroy the V1 flying bombs stored in the nearby mountain, regularly bombed our town. So I lived in a place where danger was constant, but I didn't feel all this violence as a danger. John Boorman's film, *Hope and Glory*, is like a soft version of what I went through. In my town, people were literally starving, dead bodies were scattered around the streets, windows would blow out all over us at dinner as the bombing started and planes crashed in flames on top of houses. I can even remember picking up grenades and ammunition. When you are a kid, living in such a world is such a shock that it never really wears off... I think it's the origin of my adult fascination with violence.

At the age of 26 you almost became a minister. What happened to you?

P.V.: I was in a terrible state and in the middle of a very serious psychological and economic crisis. I didn't know where I was going, but I knew

I didn't want to become a maths teacher. I really believed I was getting messages from God and my vocation was to be a preacher. I thought Christ spoke through my mouth. My then-girlfriend [my now-wife] was pregnant at the time. When she had an abortion, my economic problems vanished. So did my faith.

Why did you choose to become a filmmaker instead of pursuing your studies in science?

P.V.: I abandoned science because I felt I couldn't be extremely creative in that — I wasn't just good enough. I felt with filmmaking or painting I could express myself better. I spent eight years at the university. I studied mathematics and physics, but mostly mathematics. I was specialized in the theory of relativity. I got my PhD and then I was drafted and went in the Navy. So I never really was a physicist.

Why did you decide to leave Europe and move to the United States after Flesh + Blood?

P.V.: When I started working on *Flesh + Blood*, I was living in Holland. My plan was to use American money from studios and make movies in english that would work for the American market. That way I didn't have to move to the USA — I didn't want to live there. So I made *Flesh + Blood* and it came out in Europe in the summer of 1985 as well as in California. [And when the movie failed to reach any audience] I realized that I had made a compromise, that you couldn't make an American movie and stay in Europe. If I wanted to do American movies, I had to go and stay there. So I became an American. It was one of the biggest decision of my life, as important as the one I took when I made the decision of becoming a movie director instead of an engineer — I made that decision when I was a Navy officer. You can't make American movies if you stay in Europe because it's such a different mentality. Even Polanski can't reach out the American sensibility now that he is in Europe though he is one of the most gifted filmmaker I know and has enormous possibilities to adapt himself to anything. *Frantic* or *Pirates*, which were pretending to be American movies, were not. When he was doing *Chinatown* or *Rosemary's Baby*, which were successes, he was living in the USA.

Verhoeven: "I thought Christ spoke through my mouth." (Illustration: *Spetters*)

Verhoeven directing *The Marine Corps*, his 23-minute rehearsal for *Starship Troopers*.

How fond of science fiction are you?

P.V.: The fact that I directed sci-fi movies has confused a lot of people. I was a fan of sci-fi when I was a kid, when I was 8 or something. I was reading all the stories about Mars. I loved Flash Gordon. But as I got older I lost my interest for it. I really do prefer thinking about real things. I'm constantly reading about the Crusades, Jesus, the beginning of Christianism, the Egyptians, Hitler, World War II...

World War II had a great influence on **Starship Troopers,** *I believe...*

P.V.: The night landing of the ships on Klendathu is indeed a Normandy landing [1]. The land is not flat — it's three-dimensional — but it is that kind of feeling. Normandy was the defining moment for landing on sea — for landing anyway. When the Allies landed in Normandy, they knew that there was a very strong German presence on the coast. So they had to calculate how many waves they needed to get to the dunes and establish beachheads. They knew that the first waves would be wiped out, that the losses would be as high as 80%. The generals at that time knew that they needed this landing — even if it meant losing a great number of men — in order to be able to get the full number that they needed to beat the Germans on the ground later. And that's what they did.

What's real and what's not according to you?

P.V.: Scientifically, there is no such thing as one reality. There are many versions of reality which exist at the same time. This is a principle I consider fundamental in my life and therefore in my films. In *Showgirls* for example, Zack, Cristal and Nomi are all three convinced they control the game, and each of them is right from their point of view. The three realities live in the same story even though none of them is quite real.

---

(1) The documentary Verhoeven made for the tercentenary of the Dutch Marine Corps while in the army served also as an inspiration for *Starship Troopers*. Verhoeven: "The way they are going in and out of the boats during the landing on Klendathu and the way the Marines ran on the island of Texel in the North Sea in *The Marine Corps* are very much alike. I used even similar shots."

How do you feel about women?

P.V.: I think I have high respect for women. I think they're really strong, intelligent and a lot of fun to work with. In my personal life, I don't look for love relationships that are extremely antagonistic. The relationships with the women of my life have always been pleasant. I'm really looking for a certain partnership in love and some equality. I don't need the fight at all. I have enough fights in my work life. I want to find people that can accept me so I can accept myself. I wouldn't go with a woman who is dangerous. Artistically I can understand that, but my work is not my life.

How influential is your wife, Martine Tours, when you try to make up your mind?

P.V.: I decided to do *RoboCop*, which I first rejected finding it stupid, because of her. Martine convinced me to do *Basic Instinct* and to work with Schwarzenegger too. We are really discussing everything. I think I have a real partnership with her.

What kind of man do you think you have become?

P.V.: Basically I'm a more realistic or pessimistic or cynic person. I would not be able to do *Turkish Delight* anymore. I no longer have the naïveté or the innocence to do that. I don't have the optimism to do that. That's all gone. Politics was not something of interest to me when I was in Holland whereas in my last movies, *Showgirls* included, there are much more political statements about morals, or the politics of the United States, or what the human being is about. The movies I made in Europe are about people but with no statements underneath. I'm no longer the person that left Holland anymore. Neither am I the person that started his career with *Business is Business* or *Turkish Delight*. I was 30 then. Now I'm 60. Thirty years of thinking and evolution or degradation or corruption of my brain have passed. For better or for worse. ■

Verhoeven: "I'm no longer the person that left Holland." (Illustration: *Turkish Delight*)

"I fuck better than God himself!"

(Eric in Turkish Delight)

People think you are a misogynist, that you just show tits and ass because nudity sells?

P.V.: What a woman shows when she shows her breasts is her instinct for reproduction. Most people like to see tits and ass just because it stimulates their sexuality, their instinctive need to mate in order to procreate. Many women like to show their body off, to offer a glimpse of their legs or to emphasize their breasts. Unconsciously, they use their sexual power to attract men to have children with. It's a biological fact, a natural law. We must accept these facts. We are sexed mammals for whom reproduction and everything pertaining to it is essential.

Do you think Showgirls *is pornographic?*

P.V.: *Showgirls* is not pornographic. It isn't trying to get an erection from you. It's more the contrary. This movie puts sex in such a perspective that it is anti-erotic. Sex is always used as a tool in the movie, as a possibility to get rich or to get a better job. People came to the theatres because they thought they would see a highly erotic movie, but clearly it isn't.

Your sex scenes are devoid of any carnal excitement. You can even sense danger during them.

P.V.: The sex scenes between Catherine Tramell [Sharon Stone] and Nick Curran [Michael Douglas] in *Basic Instinct* were never supposed to get exciting. They are in fact thriller scenes. They are disguised as erotic scenes but it's basically a killer-walking-into-your-house-at-night kind of scene. It doesn't mean however that I think sex is dangerous. It's just that I find interesting to use this soul surrending moment, this moment of ultimate confidence and acceptance and corrupt it with danger. It's like the ultimate betrayal. It's just a dramatic effect, basically. It makes the contrast much stronger. I think it's fun. Most of the time when directors shoot sex scenes they don't mean anything. You have two people on a bed, and they are starting to do something that every one knows everything about. Most of the sex scenes in American movies are used to show fucking and showing fucking is extremely boring. That's why I prefer to show sex for other reasons. I use sex for communication or hate or to express danger or to give a new piece of information. My sex scenes are always loaded with something else. I have used sex a lot of times as a counterpoint to trust.

Sometimes however you erase sex completely from your movies. In RoboCop for example there is no love/sex relationship between Murphy/RoboCop [Peter Weller] and Lewis [Nancy Allen].

P.V.: If I had given too much importance to their story, I would have had to drop everything about Murphy's family. And Murphy's quest for Paradise lost through the gradual recovery of his memory was so important to me that I couldn't see any other route. Maybe in a psychological film there would have been room for such a question. But in science fiction you have to take the short route. I'd even say we worked on the Lewis character in such a way that a sexual relationship between Murphy and her would be inconceivable. Let alone the fact that it could have been dangerous... People would have wondered how they could do it, as Murphy is not really equipped for that. So I had Nancy Allen cut her hair, gain quite a few pounds, put a band around her chest to flatten her breasts. She became a hard woman instead of an attractive lady.

Verhoeven: "A sexual relationship between Murphy and RoboCop would be inconceivable."

Verhoeven:
"It's normal for
Gerard to see
a homosexual Christ."
(Illustration:
The Fourth Man)

Men force most of the women portrayed in your movies into sex. Does that mean that men don't know how to deal with women?

P.V.: In a lot of cases they don't because men want to use women to satisfy their desires or their lust. Men don't want to communicate. But sex, real sex is about communication for me. Rape is an animalistic, aggressive, intruding evil behaviour. And I portray rape in my movies because I disagree. In *Hollow Man*, Sebastian [Kevin Bacon] is experiencing the power to be aggressive sexually for a little amount of time and then he goes into killing. Sexuality in his case is just a step up towards ultimate evil. Raping is bad but killing is worse in my opinion.

In The Fourth Man, you're linking homosexuality, Jesus-Christ and crucifixion. Was it a sacrilegious move on your behalf?

P.V.: It was just part of the psychology of the character of Gerard [Jeroen Krabbé]. We know from the beginning that he is a Roman-Catholic and that he is homosexual. So when he is expressing his fantasies, it's normal for this character to combine both things and see a homosexual Christ. Like women are in love with Jesus, homosexuals would be easily in love with Him too. And Gerard is. He's also in love with this young guy, Herman [Thom Hoffman], that he met in the train.

When I was a child and I saw pictures of Jesus on the cross I was always intrigued and thinking, "Why don't we get rid of the clothing so that we can see his genitals?" That's why this fantasy to see Jesus' genitals was translated into the movie [1]. Crucifixion was done naked by Romans, which means that Jesus was crucified naked. But the Catholic Church added a piece of clothing because it has always been afraid of sexuality. Taking it off was just a way to show how it should have been. But I wasn't trying to be sacrilegious.

Flesh + Blood seems to express a lot of your feelings about religion. Martin [Rutger Hauer] is using a holy statue, named St Martin, to deceive the credulity of men indeed.

---

(1) While in a church, Gerard has a vision. He sees Herman on the cross, caresses him and then takes his swimming suit off.

P.V.: We did that on purpose. It has to do with the way I see religion. In *Flesh + Blood* religion is relayed by the Cardinal [Ronald Lacey] who is an honest fellow — at least when he says he believes in signs — and by the signs God sends via Saint Martin's statue. But the statue is in fact operated by Martin — a metaphor of how divine power is used by a human being to fulfil his own ambitions. I find it amusing that Martin should survive while he has abused men's gullibility and that the Cardinal should die a victim of the very object of his life's belief and devotion. But we did not want this metaphor to be more than a metaphor. We did not try to explain what religion is.

Why is your movie about Jesus, **Christt the Man** [2]*, still in development 'hell'?*

P.V.: Because the Jesus movie is extremely complicated. I'm working on this project for the last fifteen years. Basically if you talk about Jesus you are addressing in the most direct way, in the most challenging way, in the most upsetting way millions and millions of people that are Christians. And that's really different from say *Starship Troopers*, which addresses the audience on the giant insects' level and the political level. *Starship Troopers* is not affecting your daily life, your soul. If the Jesus project works, it will have an enormous effect. It will be a new vision. Therefore you have to be much more prepared and really convinced by what you are putting on the screen. ∎

---

(2) In 1986 Verhoeven joins a group of 77 progressive theologians. Their aim: reconstructing the life of Jesus in a purely scientific way. Led by Professor Robert W. Funk, The Jesus Seminar came to the conclusion that the historical Jesus was a rebel who battled for a peaceful liberation of Israel. He cured the sick by faith healing, spent time with the outcasts and criticized Jewish religious laws. He was a charismatic speaker, spoke Aramaic and probably knew Greek and Greek philosophy. He was not of divine descent. He was a carpenter and was tried by the Jewish authorities after causing a riot. He was crucified by the Roman occupiers. No proofs of his resurrection can be found.

Verhoeven: "We did not try to explain what religion is." (Illustration: *Flesh + Blood*)

"Why photographs, if you paint?"

(Keetje in Keetje Tippel)

What do you owe to Dutch painters?

P.V.: I always felt that my movies were very close to what Dutch painters did during the 17th century [1]. If you look at Rembrandt's paintings or the works of Hyeronimous Bosch who painted a vagabond pissing against a brothel, you know that you wouldn't see that in French, Italian or English paintings. There is also this well-known painting where two people are making love in a bungalow and a dog is in the background. [When they restored the painting] they found out that there was another dog there and that he was fucking the first one. I always felt that the Dutch had always tried to portray reality as it was and even beyond that, to portray elements of reality that normally you wouldn't go for like people shitting. That sense of realism is part of our national mentality.

---

(1) For *The Fourth Man* however Verhoeven went for another approach. Since he wanted the movie to be eerie and filled with razor-sharp images, he asked Jan de Bont to mix hyper-realism painting and surrealist painting. Edward Hopper, Dali and Magritte became the main pictural influences for the movie.

Who is your favourite composer?

P.V.: Igor Stravinsky. Did you know that he was writing his scores in different colors for each instrument? His thoughts were so well organized that his scores were like works of art. The further you go into Stravinsky's music, the clearer it becomes. In art, Stravinsky might be an example. I learned more from Stravinsky than from any painters. Painters are just portraying a moment in time. Music, novels, movies are developing in time. When you start hearing music you have to follow the whole road to get to the end. The magic of the music keeps you sitting through. When you go to see a movie, it's no longer the sound but the visual that goes against time. As an artform, movies are closer from music than from painting or photography. Knowing how to catch the attention of the audience and not get them bored through a certain amount of time is one of the main achievements of these two artforms. It's the power of the artist that keeps your eyes on the screen or your ear to the orchestra. Which is really different than looking at a painting, you know. The artist doesn't need you to stay.

How influential was Sergei M. Eisenstein on your style?

P.V.: A lot of my editing techniques are based on Eisenstein editing techniques — cutting in movement, always keeping the movement floating around, fast movements of the head looking in one direction shot from a reverse angle and vice-versa and then cut in the middle of the movement to give a double switch... I used that technique during the fighting sequence between Melina *[Rachel Ticotin]* and Lori *[Sharon Stone]* in *Total Recall*. I still think that a lot of things that were invented in the 20's and 30's by Russian directors as well as other directors I still not used fully, especially in the case of Eisenstein. They have to be rediscovered.

What other directors are you found of?

P.V.: Hitchcock is certainly one of my favourite directors and I studied his work intensively, even more than the works of Fellini, Lean or Buñuel. I really like to study old masters. I like that in moviemaking, in painting...

I'm also a fan of Sam Peckinpah's work — especially his lesser known works like *Ride the High Country* [aka *Guns in the Afternoon*]. I've learned a lot watching his flicks.

What about movies?

P.V.: I'm a big admirer of old movies. I'm not looking at them everyday but there are 20 to 30 movies I consider as classics and I study them. *The Seventh Seal* is one of my favourite movies. I first saw it in Paris in 1957 or 1958. *The Seventh Seal* is one of the rare realistic approaches of medieval life. I studied *The Terminator* before I shot *RoboCop* because there was a lot of things technically that were interesting. I'm also very fond of *Metropolis*. For somebody who knows about cinema, the influence of *Metropolis* on *RoboCop* and *Total Recall* is pretty obvious.

As it is obvious that Basic Instinct *has been influenced by* Vertigo.

P.V.: When I was 18, I studied *Vertigo*. I must have seen it at least fifteen times. I know every shot of the movie by heart and entire scenes from *Vertigo* came back [in my mind] while I was shooting *Basic Instinct*. I didn't plan to do so, but as I was shooting in San Francisco I used a bridge, and it was geographically the one next to the bridge Hitchcock used in *Vertigo*. And I did the same for the car chase even if I shot it in a different way. There are a lot of parallelisms of course. When Catherine [Sharon Stone] goes to see her friend and Nick Curran *[Michael Douglas]* follows her, I asked my crew to find a church near Hazel Dobkins' house *[played by Dorothy Malone]* because I wanted to establish as a peaceful person, even if we realize later that she is also a murderer. What I didn't realize is that in *Vertigo* there is also a similar sequence with a church in the background. It is a complete unconscious gesture on my part, but it's also true that I always liked those kind of religious symbols. However *Basic Instinct* is more about the obsession of a man for a woman and how he is sexually addicted to her? It's not a romantic obsession. ■

"I want to be somebody."

(Doug Quaid in Total Recall)

How would you describe your relationship with Sharon Stone?

P.V.: The only person that I ever had a strong love-hate relationship with is Sharon Stone because we really love each other but we also really hate each other. We can really be mean to each other and we can also be very caring and wonderful to each other. When I see her it's always the same feeling and I don't want to get into that — because I would be the victim. I feel that she would be stronger ultimately because I think that she's pretty devilish herself. She would destroy me. That's why I keep a certain distance but the attraction and the rejection are very strong. I think that taking her for the lead in *Basic Instinct* was an extremely commercial powerful choice even though I was not aware of that when I did it. Nobody wanted Sharon because she was unknown, but I wanted her because I knew her from *Total Recall* and I thought that she could do it. So I pushed for her for a long time. It was the best stroke of luck that I had because I think that she added something to the movie that I think nobody else would have given me. And the fact that basically she showed whatever I asked her to show when it came to the point to show it made the movie what it is. She never complained though she was resistant. In fact she had ultimate trust that I was doing a good job. I don't think that I would have found so many actresses that would have dared to do what she did. A lot of people would have backed up, you know. I think nearly everybody would have, but she didn't. She trusted me because she felt that I was giving her the chance of her life. I brought out things in her that nobody had seen. It's the fact that nobody knew this woman that made her so extremely convincing. I think that her presence in the movie was a sensation. You can see the effect on her career. With only one movie she became a star. Now she has to find good directors. If she can fight with the director she will be fine. If the director doesn't fight she would have problems I think. Anyhow, in a year and a half, she became from a nobody the most well known actress in the United States.

How did you get along with Arnold Schwarzenegger?

P.V.: He is a very nice guy. He is probably one of the easiest actor I've ever worked with. He is not Dustin Hoffman — he doesn't have his technical and artistic level — and he knows that. Arnold will never be a stage actor because that's not where is strength is. Arnold is much more an actor in the likes of John Wayne or Charlton Heston. They are not great actors for sure but they are certainly very charismatic actors. He is very supportive of the director. If he likes the movie he will really be there whenever you need him. Arnold has no ego. You can tell him: "What you are doing is terrible!", and he will answer you: "Explain me what so bad about it?" Then you just have to replay the scene for him, show him that what he does doesn't work and he'll redo the scene. The film was so difficult that without Arnold it would have been impossible to finish it.

Rutger Hauer and you never worked again together after Flesh + Blood. What happened between the two of you?

P.V.: I still think that Rutger was the best choice for the part if he had been in a different state of mind. I first worked with him in 1969, on *Floris* — a family oriented medieval adventure series broadcasted on Dutch TV.

Verhoeven: "Arnold is much more an actor in the likes of John Wayne."

Verhoeven: "Rutger was my spokesman; he passed on my feelings." (Illust.: *Flesh+Blood*)

Then Rutger won recognition in the United States with *Soldier of Orange*. The trouble with *Flesh + Blood* was we shot it after he had done *LadyHawke*. Originally we were to shoot our film before Richard Donner's, but we had to postpone it for a year. So there was Rutger, hoping to become a major star in the States thanks to the so very romantic *LadyHawke*, and without any pause launching into another but completely opposite medieval part, all violent and negative! He didn't know where he was. Building an image there and tearing it down here... He was getting schizoid as he always puts his entire heart into his work. He could not have a clear vision of what being in *Flesh + Blood* would imply for him. So we spent all our days shouting at each other — not to mention that we had to do it in English, still a foreign language for both of us — even if every evening we were both enthusiastic about the dailies. There was something special between the two of us — see how many films we did together... A non-sexual love affair, I'd say. He was my spokesman; he passed on my feelings, my philosophy. I remember an interview David Lean gave for his 78th birthday in which he talked about his relationship with Alec Guinness. Every single night he would come back to his hotel in tears, as he could not obtain what he wanted from Guinness. Nevertheless he would choose him for his films whenever he could even though they did not agree on how they envisioned the character. In fact there was between them a mutual respect that pushed their differences aside and allowed them to get to a better result. I agree with David Lean — I tend to think such a tension may be necessary to create something. One should not try to avoid it but to accept it, hoping that everything will eventually turn out well.

Since **The Fourth Man** *you never worked again with Jeroen Krabbé whereas you both work in the United States. Any reason?*

P.V.: It just didn't happen. If you look at the movies I've done I don't know in which ones exactly I could have given him a part. Jeroen in the movies he made in the USA has been used as a villain or as a foreigner. You cannot sell Jeroen Krabbé as a complete American because of his accent unless you're doing a James Bond like movie or *The Fugitive*. There was never an opportunity to work with Rutger Hauer either because the stories I shot were not made for him. I think that both Jeroen Krabbé or Rutger Hauer could have done *Total Recall* for example, but the part that they could have played would have been the lead and it was already given to Arnold Schwarzenegger even before I came on board. They could have also played Nick Curran's character in *Basic Instinct* but the movie was already casted even before I entered the arena. On top of that Jeroen and Rutger don't live in the United States which is a big negative for the studio heads because they want people that are highly visible.

You had a pretty rough ride with Joe Eszterhas on Basic Instinct?

P.V.: The first meeting I had with Eszterhas and Michael Douglas wasn't successful although I thought it had been. Because they are a couple of pretty open sex scenes in the script I told Eszterhas that with my Dutch background of realism I would show probably a bit more than he was expecting. And he didn't like that. So when Michael and I went for holidays, Joe went behind our back to Carolco and said that he was convinced that I would make a pornographic movie out of it and that he didn't want to work in that direction. He told them that he wanted his script back. Carolco refused and Joe walked out of the movie. I have worked in the film industry for thirty years and I've always been very happy to work with writers. In both projects *RoboCop* and *Total Recall* I had the writers always with me on the set. I'm really a believer in working together with the original writer, but in this case and at that time, because of his maneuvering, he just made it impossible [See page 18 for more]. We finally ironed the issue and we went to do *Showgirls* together.

For a long time you have worked with Gerard Soeteman even on American projects.

P.V.: We had a pretty good relationship even if we didn't agree on everything. We worked together for more than fifteen years indeed. Besides we re-teamed recently. We have just finished an adaptation of

(to be followed on page 65)

Blonde Greet [Ronny Bierman] is getting married. Is that so?

Even though Eric [Rutger Hauer] and Olga [Monique van de Ven] had a good time...

...Eric dreams of murdering her [above] now that she has left him.

Keetje [Monique van de Ven] and Mina [Hannah de Leeuwe] satisfying a client.

Erik [Rutger Hauer], the hero, and Alex [Derek de Lint], the traitor, dancing the tango.

Initiation time for freshers Jacques [Dolf de Vries], Erik and Alex.

Shock treatment for Rien [Hans van Tongeren], above, and Eef [Toon Agterberg], below.

Gerard Reve [Jeroen Krabbé], below, a gay writer living out all his fantasies.

Agnes [Jennifer Jason Leigh], the bride, in the hands of Martin's mercenaries.

Martin [Rutger Hauer] and Agnes, a true love-hate relationship.

Stephen [Tom Burlinson] doesn't want to get off Martin's back.

RoboCop ●1987

RoboCop searching for memories Dick Jones [Ronny Cox] doesn't want to see disclose.

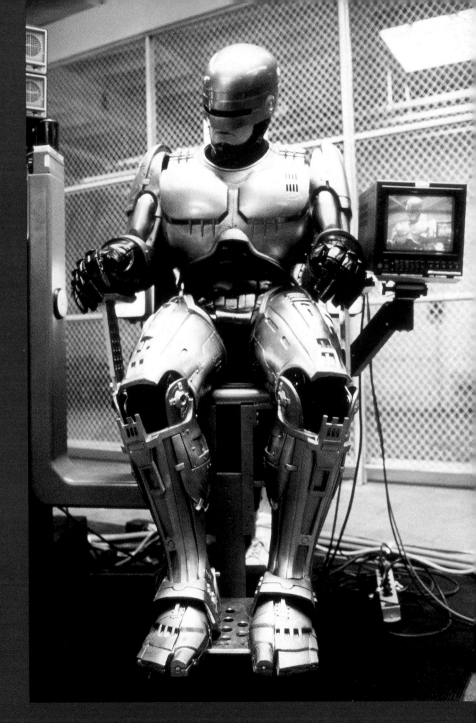

RoboCop/Murphy [Peter Weller]: creature, cyborg or machine?

Total Recall ●1990

The Mutants are looking for the air Cohaagen are depriving them off.

Doug Quaid [Arnold Schwarzenegger] doesn't want to recall.

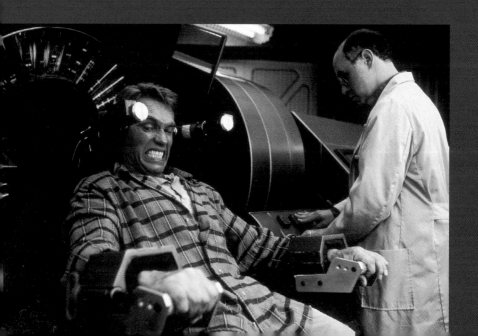

Catherine Tramell [Sharon Stone] is picky and Nick Curran [Michael Douglas] knows it.

Nomi Malone [Elizabeth Berkley], star of Goddess and immoral go-getter.

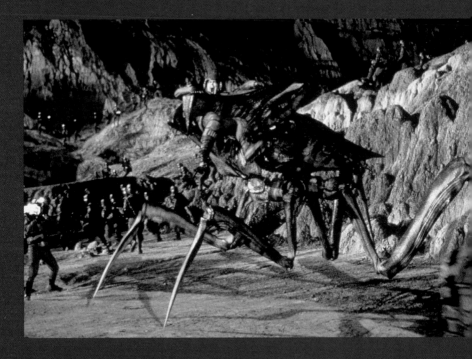

Lesson Number 1: don't mess with the arachnaids.

Johnny Rico [Casper van Dien] doesn't like to be bugged.

Sebastian [Kevin Bacon] and Linda [Elizabeth Shue] playing gods and monsters.

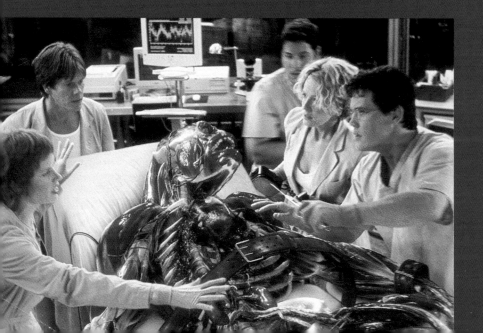

(follow up from page 48)

Guy de Maupassant's *Mont-Oriol*. It took some time because the screenplay had to be translated from Dutch to English. Ultimately I had to find an American screenwriter — the translation didn't work out indeed — to do a kind of an Americanization of what he had written in Dutch. To make something appropriate for the American market you have to write it in a certain style that basically isn't Gerard's style. Now we are going to see if that project is going to interest European producers and then American producers. For the last two years I've been trying to set up a project situated in European history to get away from the sci-fi action oriented movies I've been doing in America and I'm pretty much fed up with.

You've only worked with two directors of photography [DP], Jan de Bont and Jost Vacano. What did you find in them you couldn't find in any other director of photography?

P.V.: I'm sure I can find in America ten other DPs I could work with, but I haven't done it because I would feel lame, because I don't have the energy to look for other possibilities. First of all I wish I could still work again with Jan de Bont. I had a very good co-operation with him. The movies I did with Jan are really different looking than the movies I did with Jost. But Jan is not available anymore[1]. In fact it's clear that for one of my next movies I would like to work with another DP because I don't want to work with the same DP all the time. I want to be able to switch from Jost to another DP. In the past I used to work with two DPs and go back and forth from one to the other like Ingmar Bergman or Sergei Eisenstein did their whole life.

You're very faithful to your editors...

P.V.: I've basically worked with two editors in America: Mark [Goldblatt] and Frank [J. Urioste], who did *Basic Instinct, Total Recall* and *RoboCop*. I'd always admired Mark's work on movies like *Terminator 1 & 2* and *True Lies*. Once I've finished shooting I give him everything and I'm pretty

(1) He is now directing movies and made two hits: *Speed* and *Twister*.

much stay behind. I don't look at dailies much, either. I like to see what he'll do with it first. On the set you lose your perspective indeed. There may be takes I prefer but generally his cut will be the one I use. It's rare that I'll interfere and want something totally different. And this is how I work with everyone in postproduction. I've always felt that the postproduction process should be as collaborative as possible.

You worked twice with Rob Bottin [one of the most gifted make-up artist in Hollywood] on RoboCop and Total Recall. How implicated was he in the creative process?

P.V.: Bottin was involved in *Total Recall* from the very beginning. And a lot of things that you see in *Total Recall* are coming from him. In fact when Arnold Schwarzenegger is hidden in the fat lady and she opens up, that's his idea. And he developed it himself even at the stage of the screenplay. The idea of the guy [Kuato] that is growing outside of George was changed completely by Rob. He brought it from the back — where he was originally located — to the front adding the arms and the whole thing. So there has been an enormous amount of creativity brought by Rob in the picture. It was a very strong creative co operation between him and I. On *RoboCop*, Rob and I argued a lot about the costume. His first design was 90% perfect, but I wanted it to be 100% perfect. Then it went completely in the wrong direction. The original idea was nearly strangled. Eventually we sort it out. I think he is the most talented special effect guy in his field that I know of in Hollywood. He is not always very easy to work with. Because he is so precise and he wants everything to be so perfect he will sometimes tell you: "It's ready but I cannot give it to you because it needs to be improved" which is of course pretty difficult [to accept] when you're shooting a movie and you're on a tight schedule. But apart from that I would work again with him in a minute.

You tend to have strong relationships with your producers. Be it Rob Houwer, Gijs Versluys, Jon Davison and now Alan Marshall. What are you expecting from a producer?

P.V.: In Holland the choices were limited in terms of finding a good producer. In the United States things are different. I have a certain partnership with Alan. I never had a partnership with Rob Houwer though. I worked for the first time with Alan Marshall on *Basic Instinct*. And he is the perfect producer for me because he makes sure I don't get a heart attack. He protects me against the studios. He is really good with the money and uses it in the best way. I trust him completely. If he tells me that some things are impossible I believe him. With him I really can concentrate on my work as a director. So we have a very solid relationship. I also worked in the USA with Jon Davison who produced *RoboCop* and *Starship Troopers*. I kept a very good contact with him because I think he is also a very interesting producer. ■

"I like the excitement of war."

(Erik Lanshof in Soldier of Orange)

How do you feel about violence in movies?

P.V.: Generally speaking movies are not shaping society or reality — a movie is just a mirror or a reflection of the reality around us. If movies are violent I would say it is because society is violent. When you are working in a media it is pretty normal that you pick up the signals and that you translate them into movies. But that's a good excuse too because I like violence... in movies. I think it is really different from violence in real life. It doesn't mean anything. It is not true. Nobody is killed. Nobody is hurt. And I think it is probably worse to kill animals and eat them than to kill people in a movie. But I'm not a vegetarian either!

Flesh, blood, guts, popping eyes, bleeding wounds, dismemberments are some of the shocking images one can see throughout your movies. But the effects of Hollow Man *might be the harshest of your career.*

P.V.: *Time* magazine thought they were too. They are off-putting and disturbing to some people. I was really amazed when I heard that people were really disturbed by the effects, that they had really a problem seeing the skin disappear. I thought it was great but perhaps my sensibility is different. They are based on *écorchés* that are in a museum in Florence — my daughter found that museum. At the time I got the script in my hand she told me of that museum and got me a book with photographs in it. I showed it to my special effects supervisor, Scott Anderson. He went over there and shot a lot of photographs. And we used them for the artistic concept of the inside of the body, when the skin goes, when you see the muscles and the heart beating. That fascinates me. These wax figures I saw on photographs were so beautiful and so dramatic that it really got me into digitally re-created them. I wanted them to move. I thought it would be extremely interesting to see a human body without skin because I think it is beautiful. I'm very interested in the inside of the body, how it works, the muscles. There is a lot of opening of the human body in my movies, a lot of deterioration of the human body, falling apart. I'm very sensitive to the weakness and the vulnerability of the human body.

Why are you adopting a non-judgemental attitude at the end of Soldier of Orange?

P.V.: The message here is that these two guys who are coming from such different worlds — one is a hero [Erik/Rutger Hauer], the other one a coward [Jacques/Dolf de Vries] — are still toasting together to the future, and that's basically my way of saying: "I don't know which life-style was the best. Should you be a war hero and have all your friends killed because of your audacity? Or should you be this student who didn't do anything and who prepared himself to be a good member of society namely a lawyer or a judge?" There is nothing to condemn in there. They are equal in frame.

What's Good and what's Evil according to you?

P.V.: According to Nietzsche we are beyond that, aren't we? There is no longer Good and Evil. In fact I don't know what Good and Evil are. I don't know if there is a real distinction. It's the perspective really that counts, that gives you the feeling that there is frontier. There are certain things however that I would not do because they are against my beliefs. I would

Toasting to the future... Or to the past? (Illustration: *Soldier of Orange*)

not do a movie that is making a pro-fascist statement because I don't feel that way. That would be my frontier between Good and Evil. Nevertheless I could portray a pro-fascist character without destroying him. I have no problem with that at all and that would not offend me at all. I started my TV career in Holland with a documentary about Mussert [entitled *Portrait of Anton Adriaan Mussert;* See page 14 for more]. It was extremely controversial in Holland because I portrayed him in a neutral light. I was not condemning him, I was just showing who he was and saying, "This is a life on Earth, I have no comment." So for me the boundaries between Good and Evil don't exist artistically.

What about the end of Flesh + Blood?

P.V.: Gerard Soeteman, my screenwriter, thought Evil had won. I thought that Good had survived. He told me that perhaps it was both, like in the final scene of Roman Polanski's *The Fearless Vampire Killers* when the two protagonists escape in a cart carrying a part of the Devil with them.

You like to portray characters that live on the edge of morality. And Hollow Man seems to be quintessential of that fascination of yours.

P.V.: *Hollow Man* is a metaphor based on Plato. Plato writes in *The Republic* that a man who becomes invisible would steal on the market place, enter houses, rape women, kill men, behave like God and open prisons. Plato was using invisibility as an example for morality, to prove the very basic nature of man. According to him man is born evil and he will become evil if the constraints of society are taken away, if society cannot check him out anymore. A dictator is invisible metaphorically since he gets away with everything. In this case it's not about a dictator but about Sebastian Caine [Kevin Bacon], a flawed character. We learn from the beginning that he is not only nice and charismatic but that he can be also mean from times to times. Sebastian becomes evil because there is a shadow inside him like in all of us clearly.

Part of the controversy initiated by Starship Troopers came from the fact that you never clearly clarify throughout the movie which ideological side you embrace.

P.V.: I want the audience to clarify their position. *Starship Troopers* is a kind of cynical proposal to the audience. Or more precisely a Christian parable. If you read the parables of Jesus they are not so clear. But if you start thinking about it then you'll get the answers. Jesus used that technique at that time to put questions in your mind that you have to solve by yourself. He wanted you to participate in the process. And that's what the movie is mostly doing. It is not saying, "What they do is bad!". It is saying, "They are doing this and they are doing that... Do you want to know more? Do you really want this? Do you really participate to this idea? Or do you reject it?" I've never been much of a guy that wants to make straight statements in movies. I've never done that. *Total Recall* or *Basic Instinct* don't have any political messages. But they are certainly full of ambiguity. Like most of my work, especially in the United States.

Though ambiguous your endings are always filled with a sense of hope...

P.V.: When I was younger I read Gustav Jung who said something like: "There is Order and Chaos on Earth, and I have the careful hope that Order will prevail ultimately." That has always been a part of me. I don't know if it is true but artistically for me it is. ■

JOIN UP NOW!

THEY'LL KEEP FIGHTING

AND THEY'LL WIN!

"The only good bug is a dead bug!"

(Starship Troopers)

Do you think that with RoboCop you started your political study of the American society?

P.V.: We were just satirizing American television in *RoboCop*. The first commercial that we see in the movie is a shot-by-shot copy of a car commercial that was often aired on television while we shot the film. All these commercials were already in the original script. I did not add them. Let's say maybe I made them a bit more satirical than an American director might have.

Do you think that Total Recall *can be considered as a metaphor about the melting pot?*

P.V.: Philip K. Dick didn't dwell into political statements in his work. He is playing with schizophrenia, double reality. I read *Total Recall* like that. The dictatorship on Mars is very stereotypical. Ronny Cox, who plays Cohaagen, is really playing it like the big bad guy in a James Bond movie. He hassles freedom fighters and mostly kills them. So there is a political context but it is a very superficial and a very understandable one.

The movie is saying that basically a dictatorship in general is not good and leads to violence. That's there but it does not have any implications for American society.

What about Starship Troopers?

P.V.: *Starship Troopers* has political implications. It is really a movie about a fascist society. It's really saying that the USA has had in the past a fascist colouring and still can have a fascist colouring although it's a democracy — or pretends to be a democracy. When I did *RoboCop* I was just commenting on my direct environment, the one I had seen for a certain number of months. I was more looking at the direct level like what you see on TV. I couldn't read at that time newspapers with a suspicious eye. America often pretends that there is another goal than the one they really have. They are asking Iran to settle the issue of state government supported terrorism for example while the CIA, which is a government agency, is destroying a lot of what the leftist government was trying to achieve in Nicaragua. And Nicaragua is just one example. Ultimately it's just power politics. But there is a fascist colouring in any superpower be it the Russian superpower, be it the Aztecs in the ancient times. Basically everyone should reject all the '-isms' in the world: fascism, communism... Because these are ideological points of view and they are not true to reality or corresponding to reality. But you can certainly see how people get really seduced by these ideologies, make these choices and even accept the tragedies coming from these choices.

From commercials - RoboCop - to news reels - Starship Troopers - you seem to fear that we are heading towards a world run by an always more sophisticated propaganda.

P.V.: It is not like that in the U.S.A. yet. The newsreels in *Starship Troopers* are a hyperbole, a high exaggeration of reality — to make it clear. America is really a master in disguising its propaganda. Even in newspapers there is a tendency to be part of the government system by promoting without saying so its ideas. *Starship Troopers* points out from the beginning that the government [in the movie] uses propaganda in a very awkward way to achieve its goals. When the Kuwait War started, there

Verhoeven:
"Starship Troopers
is really a movie
about a fascist
society."

Verhoeven: *"Showgirls* is looking at the hypocrisy of sexual politics."

was an enormous amount of propaganda in the American media to prepare the American nation for this war. To get the American people behind the government and the war, the USA vilified continuously the other side. The same thing happened when Iraq nearly started again the war. You could read in the newspapers every day again more vilification of Sadam Hussain — true or untrue. The American government is basically about power but the power has strong tendencies to be economic power. It's all opening up markets ultimately. The USA is pretty much aware what opening up markets mean for the economy and they are basically using their military presence to open up these markets. It's the same in every country. Hitler did it during World War II. The war with Russia was about getting the oil fields. They didn't care about taking Leningrad or Moscow. Even when Hitler was in front of Moscow he deviated to Ukraine to get to the oil. Hitler's Germany created a department of propaganda, as you know. And even though there is no official department of propaganda in any state in the world at the moment, there is a continuous stream of propaganda coming from governments to infiltrate the press and have the press behind them as much as possible.

How political a movie is Showgirls *according to you?*

P.V.: *Showgirls* is looking at the hypocrisy of sexual politics. The movie uses Las Vegas as a kind of a symbol to portray the elements of decadence in the United States. *Showgirls* exposes an area in the United States where a lot of Americans go to, but that they don't acknowledge as existing. Vegas is like a hidden sin city. That's why *Showgirls* was badly received. I think it's a very elegant and provocative movie. It's the best documented movie that I've done in the United States. The story is to a certain degree fictitious of course, but the elements we used are based on real facts. Basically the way Vegas works is not different from what you see in the movie which is basically a complete continuous using of sex to make money. People think *Showgirls* in shocking… But to me, it isn't. ■

"I got one interest here. And that's the show."

(Tony Moss in Showgirls)

What parts of the moviemaking process do you like the most?

P.V.: The shooting itself, generally speaking, is an unpleasant, harsh process that I don't like. It requires a lot of suffering from the part of the director and certainly from the part of the other people too. You're working under high tension and high pressure and this applies even more so when you're making big logistic movies like *Total Recall* or go for stars like Sharon Stone or Michael Douglas. There are so many tensions: budget tension, logistic tension, special effects tension, the stars that you cannot handle... I mean you can do it but you constantly seem to lose your grip on the movie. I still enjoy doing the casting, the storyboarding, as well as working on the production schedules, the editing, the music though. Shooting a movie is like walking a marathon or having to go through an operation. The first couple of times, when I was working for TV, I was naive and I didn't know all the dangers that were hanging over my head. I was much more relaxed. But I'm never relaxed anymore. I'm always tense. Perhaps because I'm overreaching, I'm always trying to get things that are beyond my possibilities. I always push the limits. I try to do things that I have not done before, that are dangerous, overwhelming and challenging. I want every movie to be an adventure but I can't handle that adventure so well psychologically. If I were more confident or stronger, I would enjoy it more, but I don't. As the years passed I've become a really different person, driven, unpleasant...

Do you enjoy fighting with actors [1]?

P.V.: I don't think that confrontation is a way to be artistic. I don't believe that at all. It's just that I want the movie to be acted my way. I want the actors to follow my vision. I have a vision of how they should look, how they should behave, how they should talk, how they should walk. And *Basic Instinct* is a very strong example of that. The movie was so stylised that the actors were not immediately willing to go my way. I had to force them. I had to fight with them. I mean I'm sitting there to get what I want and whatever is necessary I do. I'm not a manipulator however. I won't say this to achieve that. I just say, "This is what I want." It's very Hitchcockian you know.

Does that mean that no one on the set can interfere with your vision of the movie?

P.V.: The clearer my vision of the movie is, the more fanatically I'm trying to get it. I want everything exactly like I had them in mind and if the cameraman doesn't do it the way I want, then I'll be upset and I will fight to get what I want.

The more you make movies, the more linear they get.

P.V.: At the beginning of my career, it was difficult for me to have in mind more than 20 to 30 minutes of my movie. But now that I'm older I can foresee the whole structure and I'm much more able to make complex movies. I'm building complete symphonies. I'm able to play the piano,

---

(1) Verhoeven is also fond of real-time acting. Rob Bottin: "First Paul reads a scene from the script and what he consequently puts on film never lasts longer on the screen than the time it takes him to read the scene in paper form. In other words, Paul uses only real time; he does not draw anything out." (*in* Paul Verhoeven, *Faber & Faber*)

Verhoeven: "I want actors to follow my vision." (Illustration: Shooting of *Basic Instinct*)

do a quartet and use counterpoint at the same time. And I achieved that with *Basic Instinct*. I even made a graphic representation of the different lines and the different levels of tensions. It was like a score.

When you read screenplays do you tend to evaluate them in terms of men and women?

P.V.: My reading is independent of that. For *Total Recall* I only realized later that it was full of men. I chose *RoboCop* ultimately because of the story. I didn't care if it was a male or a female, and if the female part was so small. In fact I really realized all of that when I did the casting.

What are the limitations imposed by a period piece?

P.V.: You have to shoot reality in a reduced way. You cannot move the camera in another street unless you have set it beforehand. You cannot be inspired by the moment and let the camera float around. So you're always reducing your possibilities.

For some camera movements you're using a gyroscope camera. What kind of feeling do you get with it?

P.V.: My German cameraman, Jost Vacano, invented it. It's a camera that you can hold in your hands [he created that camera for *The Boat*]. It follows the movements of your thumbs and your elbow. Instead of putting on the ground a dolly, I use it now to make tracking shots. The only inconvenience is that this camera isn't blimped so you can't record any direct sound. All the dialogs have to be looped afterwards. I used it for the first time on *Spetters* [the story of three blue collars only interested in sex, girls and motorcycles]. *Spetters* had no storyboards [2]. I was just walking on the set and working a bit with the actors, then the cameraman was brought in and we started shooting. *Spetters* was shot in a very free way. Whatever we thought of, we did. I just gave these young actors all the freedom I could. If anyone wanted to walk here or there, I was always saying, "OK, we'll follow you." It gave the movie a really dynamical dimension. ∎

---

(2) Usually Verhoeven tends to create storyboards and draw them for all his movies.

Verhoeven: "*Spetters* was shot in a very free way." (Illustration: Shooting of *Spetters*).

"I am what I always wanted to be."

(Martin in Flesh + Blood)

Even if we share the destiny of your characters you don't allow us to feel for them or pity them. Do you agree?

P.V.: I'm looking biologically at my characters, like if I were studying flies. There is indeed a certain distance when treating my characters. As an artist I'm not compassionate or manipulative like some American directors are. I don't try to make you cry. I never do that because I feel it's not art but manipulation, playing with your emotions like a national anthem or something like that. I feel very close in the way I'm expressing emotions to the composer Igor Stravinsky. His way of expressing emotions is not on the surface like Puccini. There is a distance and I personally love that. It gives the audience the possibility to look at everything through a dark mirror, let's say. I don't allow the audience to really and completely touch these emotions. I keep them hidden and the audience has to see them through the construction of the script. I don't go for *Erin Brockovich* kind of movies. I'm on the opposite side. I don't put the emotions in your face; I don't make them obvious to your eyes. I give away my emotions to the audience always a little bit later, slower and they may even don't get them when they see the movie for the first time.

You really enjoy portraying strong female characters.

P.V.: That's clear. Carmen [Denise Richards] in *Starship Troopers* is very different from Catherine Tramell [Sharon Stone] in *Basic Instinct* however. With Carmen I wanted to show a modern woman. She is emancipated. And she is more interested in her career than in her lovelife. Her feelings for Johnny aren't strong enough to overcome her wish to become a super pilot. Carmen is really a woman on the way to the top, a kind of ambition women were not allowed to follow in the last couple of hundred years. Catherine Tramell is the Devil. She's a human being, fully human, but she's also devilishly divine. The fact that she didn't kill Nick Curran [Michael Douglas] at the end doesn't mean that she won't kill him. She will anyhow. He's a dumb guy and she's in control. You cannot beat the Devil. Originally, I wanted *Sympathy for the Devil* from The Rolling Stones in the movie, but it didn't work.

Eric, the main character of Turkish Delight, *is a romantic character but a very obsessed one as well. How do you analyse his last gesture?*

P.V.: Olga [Monique Van de Ven], his girlfriend, is dead. It's over. She's gone and now other things will happen. So Eric [Rutger Hauer] doesn't have to bring the wig [1] back home as a relic, as an expression of his sadness. He walks outside with the wig in his hands, puts it in a garbage can and then goes away. We stay on the wig but it's also meaning that life is stronger.

Keetje Tippel [Monique van de Ven] and Nomi Malone [Elizabeth Berkley] share the same story: they fuck their way up.

P.V.: The character of Keetje Tippel interested me because I was able to portray how sexuality at the end of the 19th century was ruling the day. That's the same situation clearly in *Showgirls* although Nomi is more driven by ambition while Keetje Tippel is more driven by the terrible circumstances she has to get out of or to get her family out of. The fact that she has to prostitute herself is more imposed on Keetje. Nomi on the

---

(1) Because she had to endure chemotherapy Olga became bold.

Hans Van Tongeren [Rien], Verhoeven, Renée Soutendijk [Fientje] shooting *Spetters*.

contrary has decided to use the business of sexuality. You could also argue that Nomi is in fact closer to Fientje [the character played by Renée Soutendijk in *Spetters*] than Keetje. Fientje uses her sexual possibilities to try to upgrade herself from the French fries towards a better existence indeed. And that's what Nomi is trying to do as well. I don't think Fientje is ever in love with any of the three boys. She picks out the most promising one of this group of people, Rien, and uses her body to make a deal for him. She clearly promises and suggests to the journalist Frans Henkhof [Jeroen Krabbé] that he will be able to fuck her if he can have Rien sponsored by a Japanese motorcycle company. And Nomi goes continuously through the same kind of areas when she promises or gives her body to Cristal [Gina Gershon] or Zack [Kyle MacLachlan], the manager of the Stardust. The two characters share a lot of similarities. But of course it's also obvious that all three women, Keetje, Fientje and Nomi, have a similar response to society. They are all saying: "OK. I don't have a special talent, I'm not highly intelligent but I have a swell body and I can use it to get where I want to go."

How would you define the relationship between Erik [Rutger Hauer] and Alex [Derek de Lint] in Soldier of Orange? Does Fyodor Dostoevsky's The Brothers Karamazov had any influences on their portrayal ?

P.V.: I have no idea. I read it when I was 23-year old or something. It had certainly a strong influence on my thinking. It's possible that this book has influenced *Soldier of Orange*, but I certainly didn't think about it while doing the movie. The important thing about Erik and Alex and their relationship is that though they are on the opposite side of the political spectrum — one goes for the resistance, Erik, and the other one goes for the German army and becomes an SS officer, Alex — they are still accepting each other even after they have sided. So the statement here is that friendship is superseding political choices. And I show that when Erik [who is under the close watch of the German Secret Service] goes to see Robbie — the resistant fighter who later becomes a traitor — and suddenly sees his friend Alex as a German soldier on his way to the Eastern front. They recognize themselves, smile and wave at each other although they chose different paths. For me that was what an important part of the movie was about.

Rien [Hans van Tongeren] in Spetters *and Johnny Rico [Casper Van Dien] in* Starship Troopers *have a lot in common, don't you think?*

P.V.: Yes, they have. They are caught in their environment and try to break out of it. Rien in *Spetters* tries to get out because he has this talent for motocrossing that will lead him to the top. And once at the top, he will have a status, he will no longer be this guy among 50 million other people. He will be part of the top 100. But he has an accident, falls back and kills himself because he can no longer live in this cloistered environment. In *Starship Troopers*, Johnny Rico is caught in his political environment and doesn't seem to be able to look through that. It doesn't know that the bugs are just retaliating to the colonization of their planet by Mormon extremists. He might not even be able to understand it. He takes up the "Join up now!" cry literally. And by the end of the movie he has found his place and stays within the machine.

There's no such thing as a proper hero in Flesh + Blood...

P.V.: If you follow Martin [Rutger Hauer] and see him as a likeable guy, it's precisely because you're aware that his actions are not those of all the cliché heroes you always see on the big screen. I deliberately chose the contrary of what is traditionally done in fairy tales or adventure films. If you take medieval fables — King Arthur or Indiana Jones, the heroes survive because they are 'good'. Bullshit! We wanted true-to-life characters. That's why we made them as a combination of Good and Evil.

How different and/or similar according to you are Christine Halslaag [Renée Soutendijk] and Catherine Tramell?

P.V.: It's basically the same character. *Basic Instinct* is an Americanization of *The Fourth Man*.

Murphy/RoboCop [Peter Weller] isn't for you just a comic book figure. You wanted this character to go beyond that.

P.V.: Murphy's tranformation into RoboCop is a metaphor of death. I don't want to make any comparison with Jesus but there is an obvious Christ-like symbolism in the film. *RoboCop* is the story of a resurrection.

Do you think that Doug Quaid [Arnold Schwarzenegger] is the chosen one and Murphy a martyr?

P.V.: I understand the question but I will never put it that way. If you put it in religious terms Doug Quaid is indeed the chosen one, a Messiah kind of character, who fulfils the destiny of Mars, and Murphy is a martyr. I never thought it that way however when I made it even though you can see that if you want to.

Though Dr Garner [Jeanne Tripplehorn] is one of the most intense and feverish female characters portrayed in your movies, it was completely overshadowed by the character of Catherine Tramell. Can you talk a bit about her?

P.V.: When I shot the movie the part of Jeanne Tripplehorn was as important as the part of Sharon Stone. But because of the public opinion and all the attention afterwards, all the emphasis was placed on the performance of Sharon Stone. I really feel Dr Garner is a pretty fascinating character. I spent a lot of time trying to make it as interesting as possible and I worked very hard with Jeanne on it. She is only the one that seems to have really consistent feelings for Nick Curran even if she knows that it is stupid to do so. Though she is not a shadowy character like Nick Curran or a perfidious female like Catherine Tramell, Dr Garner is not free of any flaws. She does things that ethically deserve a blame for — she gives away Nick Curran's file to the internal affairs guy. She makes mistakes but she is of course not the killer neither is she a villain or an inhuman person that doesn't care about people. She is one of the most normal people in the movie in fact. It's just because of her bisexuality and its impact that she becomes involved in all this.

How complex is Nomi's character according to you?

P.V.: Nomi is a very rich character. When Cristal [Gina Gershon] tells her, "We are all whores," she doesn't realize she has touched a very sensitive chord in Nomi, about a past she's been trying to put behind her. Nomi seems to be ready to do anything to reach her goal, yet in the last minute her morals take over. She retrieves her dignity when Molly gets raped, when she sees somebody innocent treated in such a way. She can

Verhoeven and Elizabeth Berkley [Nomi Malone] on the set of *Showgirls*.

draw a line... This is a very American vision, a fable on redemption. Redemption is a part of American mythology. It's a romantic vision of life entertained by a whole culture. Maybe it's also the symptom of an inability to cope with reality. And the movies I made in the USA are like that; they are all influenced by that vision.

What kind of life Nomi is going to choose at the end of the movie?

P.V.: She goes to Los Angeles. After doing Vegas she is going to do Hollywood. I'm saying basically that Hollywood and Vegas are the same.

Rasczak [Michael Ironside] seems to be your spokesman in Starship Troopers. *Do you agree?*

P.V.: He is my spokesman as an artist, yes. Not as a person. The fact that you can portray a fascist idiom and even create fascist beauty doesn't mean that as a person I would support a fascist regime. Being an artist permits you to identify with a certain kind of thinking while in your own social life you would dismiss that kind of thinking because you would see the felony and the ugliness of it. Look at Dostoevsky's *Crime and Punishment.* Dostoevsky goes on the path of a nihilistic anarchist criminal and makes himself a criminal though he is not a criminal himself. Clearly Raskolnikoff is Dostoevsky, but he is Dostoevsky as an artist not Dostoevsky as a human being. A lot of the things that Rasczak are standing for I would not be following. But I know that some people think that way and are followed. That's why there is this two-fold situation in *Starship Troopers.* One is saying you're all a bunch of crazy idiots because this paradigm you're living in mean you're going to die. And I illustrate that by the newsreels and at the end of the movie — when Johnny is yelling at his unit: "You want to live forever?" The other is saying that people like Carmen or Johnny accept this kind of 'beautiful fascism' which tells you that human beings should be the ruler of the universe and not insects. And that's the other layer of the movie where you see the inside of fascism and where from the inside it looks OK whereas from outside it doesn't. If you look at Nazism you see that 90% of the Germans in the thirties were accepting Hitler and the Nazis, and that were glad and happy to do so. That it all ended up in a catastrophe is something different, isn't it?

Dizzy [Dina Meyer] is the most moving character of Starship Troopers.

P.V.: Dizzy is a warm character, warmer than a lot of other female characters that I have been portraying. She joined the army because of Johnny, because she wants to be Johnny's partner 24 hours a day, on the battle-fields and in the bedroom. In Dizzy's case, I felt it would be interesting to show a non cynical character.

How do you analyse Sebastian and Linda's relationship in Hollow Man?

P.V.: Linda had a relationship with Sebastian, and she is certainly still attracted to him but she is not giving in. She made up her mind. She makes a very clear statement at some point in the movie about why she won't bed with Sebastian. When Sebastian says: "Don't you want to make love to the invisible man? Do you remember? We talked about it?" she replies: "Yes I remember, but I'm not interested because you were never there anyhow!" Meaning, when you had sex with me you were just sexually involved and after your orgasm you went back to your computer. There was no communication between them. So I'm making again a statement about this lack of communication. It's again a man driven by orgasm desires, and has looked through him and she has realized that his sexuality is based on the fulfilment of lust — not communication. And that's why, even though the sexual was fine from an animalistic biological point of view, even though he is a charismatic genius, Linda knows that from a social human communication point of view there is nothing. ■

"We struggled through. Don't ask how."

(Jacques in Soldier of Orange)

Business is Business (1971)

It was very successful in Holland. It was just a local Dutch comedy — really Dutch. It was just a possibility for me to start in the movie industry. I came from television and I got this movie offered. It was a little booklet with all kind of short stories about two prostitutes. Each of these short stories was just a collection of different anecdotes of one or two pages. Gerard Soeteman, my scriptwriter, just put them together in a kind of an order so we would have a kind of a story. I made it as good as possible. It's not a movie of my own that one has to see. I'm glad the movie was never really released outside of Holland.

Turkish Delight (1973)

Turkish Delight is a realistic portrait of a couple during the seventies. A time when everything was possible, when everybody could do what they wanted to do without being afraid of the consequences.

I wanted to do *Turkish Delight* before *Business is Business*. But my producer, Rob Houwer, didn't dare to do it at that point. The novel was based on a real story. What's interesting is that Olga dies in the book but in reality she didn't die at all. She left Jan Wolkers, the author. So underneath there was a lot of hate because he felt betrayed. He took his revenge on women in his book. Artistically, I followed the move of the book but that's not exactly how I see relationships between men and women.

Keetje Tippel (1975)

It's a variation on the Cinderella theme — the story of a young working class girl who leaves Antwerp and ends up in Paris, where she becomes at seventeen the inspirational mistress of a great painter, and later on the wife of a rich socialist.

Soldier of Orange (1977)

Soldier of Orange is about high class, rich aristocratic kids in a war situation. What I wanted to show in that film was that war is not only murderous or stupid — it is childish too. All of a sudden men become heroes and eventually believe in what they are doing.

Spetters (1980)

At that time, I was breaking up with Rob Houwer — the producer I had been working with for 10 years. For me it was like a divorce. So basically *Spetters* was like: "Fuck the past! Let's be wild! Let's forget about the aristocracy, the rich people, and go for the blue collar, the fast movements... Let's go for dirt, for mud, for shit. Let's just go down to earth." That was the feeling. I wanted to make a clean break, to catch life as it is, to blow everything away. I wanted to make such an aggressive and provocative movie that everybody will get mad at me! And indeed everybody got mad at me. The movie made a big scandal. Even now you don't see gang rapes, erections and blowjobs that very often on screen. And these were the reasons why I wanted to make the movie. I wanted to be able to shoot in close-up an erection and a blowjob. I was acting like an angry young man. When I brought the movie to the USA, a friend of mine said to me: "*Spetters* is this year what *Mad Max* was last year."

Verhoeven: "It's a variation on the Cinderella theme." (Illustration: *Keetje Tippel)*

Verhoeven: "We made up our own medieval world." (Illustration: *Flesh + Blood*)

The Fourth Man (1983)

It was a movie that we all felt would be for a limited audience, but probably would be interesting not only for Holland but also for the rest of the world. Anyhow we made the movie on a very tight budget. I shot it in 36 days, very fast. It's a movie that is really different from the rest of my work because it is much more intimate, much more atmospheric and based on acting. The shooting was like any other. We were glad once it was finished.

Flesh + Blood (1985)

We did extremely extensive research, taking as an historical basis all the information we had gathered on the period: books, sketches, drawings, paintings. We used Brueghel's paintings to design sets and private diaries from the period supplied our dialogue. Such documents gave a precise idea of spoken language at the time. We tried not to go beyond historical reality. For instance, cutting up a dead dog and throwing the pieces over the walls of a castle was very common in the Middle Ages. When warriors could not obtain victory in a siege situation they would look for dead animals, preferably plague-stricken, and they throw them over the walls in order to launch an epidemic. And the town would quickly surrender. Bacteriological warfare is nothing new! Everything that happens in the film is based upon fact. Most of the inventions of Stephen [Tom Burlinson] are inspired from Leonardo Da Vinci's sketches. All sets are realistic. But they fit into the story in a very lyrical way. Let's say we digested our datas and we made up our own medieval world.

RoboCop (1987)

I wanted action sequences as brilliantly staged as in *Rambo*, special effects as effective as in *Star Wars* — especially for ED 209, a situation reminiscent of Frankenstein, a film as satirical as Billy Wilder's. I couldn't say if I managed to reach all those goals but they were the challenge offered by the script. And I liked that challenge. Also, it was an opportunity to get familiar with such things as matte-paintings, bluescreens, miniatures...

Most of all the story corresponded with my own philosophical concerns about life and death, fear of dying, resurrection, and Paradise lost. *RoboCop* was also for me a rescue operation to get out of Europe. I saw possibilities to do it in my own way so I jumped on the occasion. If it hadn't work, I would have come back to Europe.

Total Recall (1990)

After *RoboCop* I didn't want to do a sci-fi movie and for half a year I read anything in town to see if I could do a "normal" movie. But I could not find one and the first script that I really liked was *Total Recall*. What interested me in *Total Recall* was its two different layers of reality: 1] the story about this man who finds out that he is a secret agent and people are chasing him and he is saving the entire planet at the end and 2] the fact that you could also see it as a story about a man that is dreaming all that up and ends up being lobotomized. And these two stories are indeed kind of interesting from a physical point of view.

Basic Instinct (1992)

I knew that I would be really good at making thrillers because I studied them all my life. I always wanted to do one and I couldn't find any project of that kind in Holland because it is a peaceful society. It never made much sense to do a thriller there.

Basic Instinct was supposed to get an NC-17 but got a R. If I had gotten an NC-17 we still could have released the movie, but only 30% of the theatres would have played it. So I trimmed the movie a bit and got an R [In Europe the movie was released uncut]. But the movie was still considered as outrageous by the MPAA.

Showgirls (1995)

For *Showgirls* Joe Eszterhas and I went together to Las Vegas. We spent an enormous amount of time there. We interviewed 200 people. We have pages and pages of interviews with the strip girls, the managers, and the choreographers from every big and sleazy show [in Vegas city].

Verhoeven: "What interested me in *Total Recall* was its two different layers."

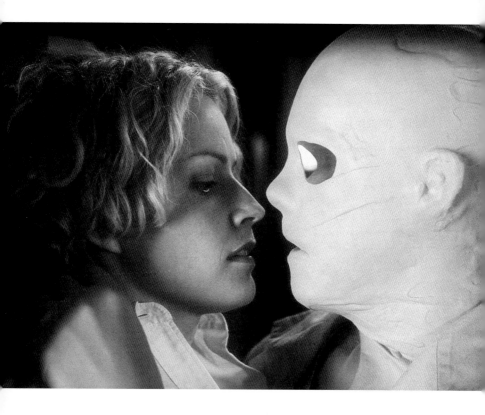

Sebastian: "Don't you want to make love to the invisible man?" (Illustration: *Hollow Man*)

We interviewed the owners of the hotels too. Then Joe wrote the story. The story built itself out of the interviews — what could be used, what couldn't... Ultimately I was involved from the beginning in this movie. So that's why the movie is so personal even from an objective point of view.

Starship Troopers (1997)

When we started around 1993/1994 to work on the project, Ed Neumeier and I, it was just a story about young adults fighting giant bugs in space. That was really the first layer. And it was the layer that made me step into the project as well as Phil Tippett. It was like a Ray Harryhausen movie. The three of us were talking about this movie even during the post-production of *Basic Instinct*. Then a lot of other elements came in. In these last years I came much more aware of American politics, and especially American foreign politics. When the movie came out, *The Washington Post*, a very political rightwingish kind of newspaper, vilified the movie to eliminate the danger it represented — it was no conspiracy however. In that article they were defending the USA and they made sure — by publishing not a review but an editorial — that all over the world people will notice because of the status of *The Washington Post*.

Hollow Man (2000)

I joined *Hollow Man* after I said to the studio that I couldn't solve the problems with the *Houdini* script. So I picked *Hollow Man* at the very end when the script was nearly done *[the script was for eight years in development]*. I added a couple of sequences like the scene with the kids in the car — I wanted an element of comedy before the rape sequence. I changed the scene of the killing of Sarah [one of Sebastian's assistant] because it was done by the invisible Sebastian and I felt it would look strange if the girl was miming her violent death. So I asked to rewrite it and to throw the blood over Sebastian so that now he gets her as a bloody guy. When the fly circles around Sebastian's head and he grabs it and kills it, I added that too. I added that because I wanted to show that he was going into evil.

"What you make of reality is far more interesting than reality itself."

(Gerard Reve in The Fourth Man)

CINEMA

1960 - ONE LIZARD TOO MANY (EÉN HAGEDIS TEVEEL)

Production Company The Netherlands Student Film Industry **Screenplay** Jan van Mastrigt **Cinematography** Frits Boersma **Editing** Ernst Winar **Music** Aart Gisolf **Cast** Erik Bree, Marijke Jones, Hermine Menalda, Hans Schneider, P.A. Harteveld **Duration** 35 mins. B&W.

Synopsis The unhappy wife of a sculptor starts an affair with a student. The student has a girlfriend who models for the wife's husband. The husband can't sculpt her wife in clay unless she takes on a different personality.

1961 - NOTHING SPECIAL (NIETS BIJZONDERS)

Production Company The Netherlands Student Film Industry **Screenplay** Jan van Mastrigt **Cinematography** Frits Boersma **Editing** Ernst Winar **Cast** Jan van Mastrigt, Marina Schapers **Duration** 9 mins. B&W.

Synopsis In a café a young man imagines that his fictitious twin is dating his girlfriend Marina.

1962 - THE HITCHHIKERS (DE LIFTERS)

Production Company The Netherlands Student Film Industry **Screenplay** Jan van Mastrigt **Cinematography** Frits Boersma **Editing** Ernst Winar **Cast** Geerda Walma van der Molen, Jaap van Donselaar, Maarten Schutte, Jan van Mastrigt **Duration** 17 mins. B&W.

Synopsis Three boys are competing for the same girl. A Studebaker might be helpful.

1963 - LET'S HAVE A PARTY (FEEST)

Production Company Paul Verhoeven Production **Screenplay** Jan van Mastrigt **Cinematography** Ferenc Kálmán-Gáll **Editing** Ernst Winar **Music** Dick Broeckaerts **Cast** Yvonne Blei-Weissmann, Dick de Brauw, Pieter Jelle Bouman, Wim Noordhoek **Duration** 28 mins. B&W.

Synopsis A 15-year old boy and a girl two years younger than him are having a romance. One day, at a party, they are forced into playing a kissing game.

1970 - THE WRESTLER (DE WORSTELAAR)

Production Company Nico Crama Production **Screenplay** Paul Verhoeven, Kees Holierhoek **Cinematography** Jan de Bont **Editing** Jan Bosdriesz **Music** J. Stoeckart **Cast** Jon Bluming, Bernhard Droog, Wim Zomer, Mariëlle Fiolet **Duration** 20 mins. Colour.

Synopsis A young man is having an affair with the wife of a feared wrestler. His father tries to warn him but he only brings more confusion.

1971 - BUSINESS IS BUSINESS (WAT ZIEN IK?)

Producer Rob Houwer **Screenplay** Gerard Soeteman, based on Albert Mol's *What's that I see?*... *Conversations with Blonde Greet* **Cinematography** Jan de Bont **Editing** Jan Bosdriesz **Music** Julius Steffaro **Set design** Massimo Götz, Henk Koster **Cast** Ronny Bierman (Blonde Greet), Sylvia de Leur (Nel), Piet Römer (Greet's Lover), Bernhard Droog (Nel's husband), Jules Hamel (Nel's pimp) **Duration** 93 mins. Colour.

Synopsis Blonde Greet and Nell are two prostitutes who enjoy their life in Amsterdam's red-light district. They are specialized in kinky and deviant sex practices. Their clients? Mostly bourgeois/upper-class men.

1973 - TURKISH DELIGHT (TURKS FRUIT)

Production Company Rob Houwer Films **Screenplay** Gerard Soeteman, based on the eponymous novel by Jan Wolkers **Cinematography** Jan de Bont **Editing** Jan Bosdriesz **Production Designer** Ralf van de Elst **Music** Rogier van Otterloo **Cast** Rutger Hauer (Eric Vonk), Monique van de Ven (Olga Staples), Tonny Huurdeman (Mother), Wim van den Brink (Father), Dolf de Vries (Paul), Hans Boskamp (Vinkelchef), Manfred de Graaf (Henry) **Duration** 112 mins. Colour.

Synopsis Eric, a young artist, has just been dumped by the love of his life. Though he engages in sex with various women he can't forget Olga and remembers their time together Some years later, they bump into each other at a train station. But Olga seems different, sick...

1975 - KEETJE TIPPEL (ib.)

Production Company Rob Houwer Films **Screenplay** Gerard Soeteman, based on the memoirs of Neel Doff **Cinematography** Jan de Bont **Editing** Jane Sperr **Production Designer** Roland de Groot **Costumes** Robert Bos **Music** Rogier van Otterloo **Cast** Monique van de Ven (Keetje Tippel), Rutger Hauer (Hugo), Eddy Brugman (Andre), Peter Faber (George), Hannah de Leeuwe (Mina), Andrea Domburg (Mother), Jan Blaaser (Father) **Duration** 109 mins. Colour.

Synopsis Keetje and her family leave Frisia with the hope of finding a better life. Once in Amsterdam, the family finds out that the basement they are going to live in is a soaking damp. To make ends meet, Mina, the older sister, starts to work as a prostitute soon followed by Keetje, who unsuccessfully tried to work in a laundry then a hat-maker's shop. But fate enters the picture and Keetje becomes a model for George, a painter. She then falls in love for Hugo, a bank clerk.

1977 - SOLDIER OF ORANGE (SOLDAAT VAN ORANJE)

Production Company Rob Houwer Films/Gijs Versluys **Screenplay** Gerard Soeteman, Kees Holierhoek, Paul Verhoeven, based on the eponymous novel by Erik Hazelhoff Roelfzema **Cinematography** Jost Vacano **Editing** Jane Sperr **Production Designer** Roland de Groot **Costumes** Elly Claus **Music** Rogier van Otterloo **Special Effects** Robert Leerinck, Aat van Westen

Cast Rutger Hauer (Erik Lanshof), Jeroen Krabbé (Guus), Edward Fox (Colonel Rafelli), Derek de Lint (Alex), Eddy Habbema (Robbie), Lex van Delden (Nico), Dolf de Vries (Jacques), Huib Rooymans (Jan), Belinda Meuldijk (Esther) **Duration** 153 mins. Colour.

Synopsis August 1938. Erik, a 'fresher', joins Leiden University's student association Minerva. With Nico, Jan, a Jewish boy, Alex, the son of a German-born mother, Jacques and Guus, the president, Erik devotes himself to courting girls and partying. But the German invasion changes his plans and Erik, along with Guus, flees to England to join the Dutch Secret Service. Alex, however, join the Dutch SS Corps. For the three of them the true adventure can begin.

1980 - SPETTERS (ib.)
Producer Joop van den Ende **Screenplay** Gerard Soeteman **Cinematography** Jost Vacano **Editing** Ine Schenkkan **Production Designer** Dick Schillemans **Costumes** Yan Tax **Music** Tom Scherpenzeel, Kayak **Cast** Hans van Tongeren (Rien), Renée Soutendijk (Fientje), Toon Agterberg (Eef), Maarten Spanjer (Hans), Marianne Boyer (Maya), Rutger Hauer (Gerrit Witkamp) Peter Tuinman (Fientje's brother) Jeroen Krabbé (Frans Henkhof) **Duration** 115 mins. Colour.

Synopsis Rien, Eef and Hans are only interested in motocrossing, girls and fast money. Fientje, a lovely ambitious French fries seller, wants to escape her depressing life. The four of them meet during a racing contest. Immediately attracted to her, Rien, the most gifted racer of the band, begins to court her. But an accident ruins his life and Fientje's hopes. Then Fientje finds out that Eef, who was bashing and stealing gays, is in fact a homo. Why not pick the dumb Hans then?

1983 - THE FOURTH MAN (DE VIERDE MAN)

Production Company Rob Houwer for United Film Company of the Netherlands **Screenplay** Gerard Soeteman, based on the eponymous novel by Gerard Reve **Cinematography** Jan de Bont **Editing** Ine Schenkkan **Production Designer** Roland de Groot **Costumes** Elly Claus **Music** Loek Dikker **Sound Effects** Floris van Manen **Special Effects** Harrie Wiessenhaan, Chris Tucker **Cast** Jeroen Krabbé (Gerard Reve), Renée Soutendijk (Christine Halsslag), Thom Hoffman (Herman), Dolf de Vries (Doctor De Vries), Geert de Jong (Ria), Hans Veerman (Begrafenisondernemer), Hero Muller (Josefs), Caroline de Beus (Adrienne) **Duration** 90 mins. Colour.

Synopsis Gerard Reve, a gay alcoholic writer, is invited to do a conference in Vlissingen. There he falls sexually for Christine Halsslag, an androgynous beauty salon owner, also treasurer of the literary association that invited him. The next day, while snooping around Christine's house, he discovers a photograph of the beautiful young guy he had fixated on at the station before taking his train to Vlissingen. He also finds out that Christine had three former husbands who all died violently. Is this all pure fate?

1985 - FLESH + BLOOD

Production Company Riverside Pictures/Orion Pictures **Screenplay** Gerard Soeteman **Cinematography** Jan de Bont **Editing** Ine Schenkkan **Production Designer** Felix Murcia **Costumes** Yvonne Blake **Music** Basil Poledouris **Cast** Rutger Hauer (Martin), Jennifer Jason-Leigh (Agnes), Tom Burlinson (Steven), Jack Thompson (Hawkwood), Fernando Hillbeck (Arnolfini) Susan Tyrrell (Celine), Ronald Lacey (Cardinal), Brion James (Karsthans), Kitty Courbois (Anna), Hans Veerman (Father George) **Duration** 126 mins. Colour.

Synopsis Betrayed by Arnolfini, a nobleman who wanted his town back, and Hawkwood, the Captain who hired them, a band of mercenaries lead by Sergeant Martin swear to take their revenge. A chance they soon get when Arnolfini maneuvers an outdoor encounter between his son, Stephen, and Agnes, the princess he wants him to marry. The ambush is a success and the loot enormous. They even capture Agnes. Raped by Martin, she becomes his bride. But the very ingenious Stephen is determined to get his beloved back whatever the cost.

1987 - ROBOCOP

Production Company Orion Pictures **Executive Producer** Jon Davison **Screenplay** Edward Neumeier, Michael Miner **Cinematography** Jost Vacano **Editing** Frank J. Urioste **Production Designer** William Sandell **Costumes** Erica Edell Phillips **Music** Basil Poledouris **Special Effects** Peter Kukan, Robert Ballack, Dale Martin **RoboCop Designer** Rob Bottin **Sequences ED-209** Phil Tippett **Cast** Peter Weller (Murphy/RoboCop), Nancy Allen (Lewis), Ronny Cox (Dick Jones), Daniel O'Herlily (the old man), Kurtwood Smith (Clarence), Miguel Ferrer (Morton), Ray Wise (Leon), Felton Perry (Johnson), Paul McCrane (Emil), **Duration** 103 mins. Colour.

Synopsis Transferred to the dangerous district of Old Detroit — to be rejuvenated by OCP, an all-powerful conglomerate — Alex J. Murphy is gunned down savagely on his first assignment. Considered as dead what is left of his body is used to create an invincible enforcer of the law baptized RoboCop. But soon RoboCop, whose past has been blanked, begins to remember pieces of Murphy's former life: his wife, his child and above all the members of the gang that killed him. RoboCop's true quest can start.

1990 - TOTAL RECALL
Production Company Carolco Pictures **Executive Producer** Mario Kassar, Andrew Vajna **Screenplay** Ronald Shusett, Dan O'Bannon, Gary Goldman, based on the short story *We can remember it for you wholesale* by Philip K. Dick **Cinematography** Jost Vacano **Editing** Frank J. Urioste **Production Designer** William Sandell **Costumes** Erica Edell Phillips **Music** Jerry Goldsmith **Visual Effects** Dream Quest Images **Special Effects** Scott Fischer **Make-up Designer** Rob Bottin **Cast** Arnold Schwarzenegger (Doug Quaid), Rachel Ticotin (Melina), Sharon Stone (Lori), Ronny Cox (Cohaagen), Michael Ironside (Richter), Marsha Bell (George/Kuato), Mel Johnson Jr. (Benny), Michael Champion (Helm), Roy Brocksmith (Doctor Edgemar), Ray Baker (McClane) **Duration** 109 mins. Colour.

Synopsis Doug Quaid, a worker, wants to go to Mars. Unable to move up to the red planet he chooses to make a virtual trip thanks to Rekall Incorporated. But the transplanted implant wakes up what seems to be his former identity, the one of a secret agent — who was working undercover for the resistance and trying to free Mars from Cohaagen's dictatorship. Shot at by his wife, chased by Cohaagen's right arm, Richter, Quaid goes to Mars to find the truth.

1992 - BASIC INSTINCT

Production Company Carolco Pictures/Studio Canal + **Producer** Alan Marshall **Executive Producer** Mario Kassar **Screenplay** Joe Eszterhas **Cinematography** Jan de Bont **Editing** Frank J. Urioste **Production Designer** Terence Marsh **Costumes** Ellen Mirojnick **Music** Jerry Goldsmith **Special Effects** Rob Bottin **Cast** Michael Douglas (Nick Curran), Sharon Stone (Catherine Tramell), George Dzundza (Gus), Jeanne Tripplehorn (Doctor Beth Garner), Denis Arndt (Lieutenant Walker), Leilani Sarelle (Roxy), Bruce A. Young (Andrews), Chelcie Ross (Captain Talcott), Dorothy Malone (Hazel Dobkins), Stephen Tobolowsky (Doctor Lamott) **Duration** 130 mins. Colour.

Synopsis Nick Curran, a driven inspector, investigates the murder of Johnny Boz, an ageing pop star who has been killed with an ice pick. While trying to find the truth, Curran falls in love with the chief suspect — the beautiful and bisexual writer Catherine Tramell.

1995 - SHOWGIRLS

Production Company Carolco Pictures/Chargeurs **Producer** Alan Marshall, Ben Myron **Screenplay** Joe Eszterhas **Cinematography** Jost Vacano **Editing** Mark Goldblatt, Mark Helfrich **Production Designer** Allan Cameron **Costumes** Ellen Mirojnick **Music** David Stewart **Choreography** Marguerite Pomerhn-Derricks **Cast** Elizabeth Berkley (Nomi Malone), Gina Gershon (Cristal Connors), Kyle MacLachlan (Zack Carey), Glenn Plummer (James Smith), Robert Davi (Al Torres), Alan Rachins (Tony Moss), Gina Raverra (Molly Abrams), Lin Tucci (Henrietta Bazoom), Greg Travis (Phil Newkirk), William Shockley (Andrew Carver) **Duration** 131 mins. Colour.

Synopsis Nomi Malone, a sexy blonde fleeing from her past, wants to make it as a dancer in Vegas. Molly, a dressing woman, helps her out and introduces her to Cristal Connors, the star of the Stardust. But Cristal humiliates her and Nomi leaves furious. While waiting for her breakthrough, Nomi has to work as a stripper at the Cheetah. One night, Cristal buys her for Zack, her boyfriend and the manager of the Stardust. The next day, Nomi gets to audition for *Goddess*, the hit show from the Stardust.

1997 - STARSHIP TROOPERS
Production Company Big Big Pictures for TriStar/Buena Vista Int. **Producer** Alan Marshall, Jon Davidson **Screenplay** Edward Neumeier, based on the eponymous novel by Robert Heinlein **Cinematography** Jost Vacano **Editing** Mark Goldblatt, Caroline Ross **Production Designer** Allan Cameron **Costumes** Ellen Mirojnick **Music** Basil Poledouris **Creature Visual Effects Supervision** Phil Tippett **Special Effects** John Richardson **Prosthetic Make-up Supervision** Kevin Yagher **Creature Animatronics** Tom Woodruff, Alec Gillis **Cast** Casper Van Dien (Johnny Rico), Dina Meyer (Dizzy Flores), Denise Richards (Carmen Ibanez), Jake Busey (Ace Levy), Neil Patrick Harris (Carl Jenkins), Michael Ironside (Jean Rasczak), Clancy Brown (Sergeant Zim), Seth Gillian (Sugar Watkins), Patrick Muldoon (Zander Barcalow) **Duration** 135 mins. Colour.

Synopsis Though Earth is engaged in a terrifying war against alien bugs, Johnny Rico's only interest is his schoolmate, Carmen Ibanez. When she decides to join the army to become a pilot in the Star Fleet, Johnny applies for the infantry. There he learns how to be a soldier the hard way. When Johnny is about to give up, his hometown, Buenos Aires, is erased from the map by a meteor sent by the bugs. With the help of Dizzy Flores — who is secretly in love with him, Johnny vows then to take revenge and fight the bugs on their planets.

2000 - HOLLOW MAN
Production Company Columbia Pictures **Producer** Douglas Wick, Alan Marshall **Screenplay** Andrew W. Marlowe **Cinematography** Jost Vacano **Editing** Mark Goldblatt **Production Designer** Allan Cameron **Costumes** Ellen Mirojnick **Music** Jerry Goldsmith **Special Effects Supervision** Scott E. Anderson, Craig Hayes **Special Effects** Sony Pictures Imageworks Inc., Tippett Studio **Cast** Elisabeth Shue (Linda McKay), Kevin Bacon (Sebastian Caine), Josh Brolin (Matthew Kensington), Kim Dickens (Sarah Kennedy), Greg Grunberg (Carter Abbey), Joey Slotnick (Frank Chase), Mary Randle (Janice Walton), William Devane (Doctor Arthur Kramer) **Duration** 112 mins. Colour.

Synopsis Sebastian Caine, a brilliant and arrogant scientist, wants to break the molecular code for invisibility. When he finally succeeds he hides the results from his backers — the military — to experience the formula on himself. But he cannot 'come back' and stays invisible. Even his colleague and former lover, Linda McKay, is unable to help him out. First submerged by anger and despair, Sebastian begins to experience and enjoy the whole spectrum of his new power.

Paul Verhoeven

TELEVISION

1969 - FLORIS

Production Company Max Appelboom Production **Screenplay** Gerard Soeteman **Cinematography** Ton Buné **Editing** Jan Bosdriesz **Music** Julius Steffaro **Cast** Rutger Hauer (Floris van Rosemond), Jos Bergman (Sindala), Hans Culeman (Maarten van Rossem), Ida Bons (Viola), Tim Beekman (sergeant), Ton Vos (Wolter van Odesteijn), Hans Kemna (Govert) **12 episodes of 30 mins. each broadcasted every week from October 5th till December 21st** B&W.

> **Synopsis** A young nobleman, Floris van Rosemond, and an oriental magician, Sindala, team up to fight the demons and enlighten the crowds of the 16th century.

1979 - GONE, GONE (VOORBIJ, VOORBIJ)

Producer Joop van den Ende **Screenplay** Gerard Soeteman **Cinematography** Mat van Hensbergen **Editing** Ine Schenkkan **Costumes** Yan Tax **Music** Hans Vermeulen **Cast** André van den Heuvel (Ab), Andrea Domburg (Dorien), Piet Römer (Gerben), Guus Oster (Ben), Jan Retèl (Cees), Hidde Maas (Arie), Leontien Ceulemans (Tine) **Duration** 58 mins. Colour.

Synopsis A group of World War II freedom fighters makes a promise — avenging the death of their friend whenever they found the Dutch SS who killed him.

1986 - THE LAST SCENE (EPISODE N°21 OF THE SERIES THE HITCHHIKER)

Cast Nicholas Campbell (The Hitchhiker), Peter Coyote (Alex), LaGena Hart (Leda Bidel). **Duration** 26 mins. Colour

Synopsis A director threatens his female lead to get her in the right mood for a horror movie.

DOCUMENTARIES/VARIOUS

1965 - THE MARINE CORPS (HET KORPS MARINIERS)

Production Company Multifilm **Cinematography** Peter Alsemgeest, Jan Kijser, Jos Van Haarlem **Editing** Ernst Winar **Music** H.C. van Lijnschoten **Duration** 23 mins. Colour.

1968 - PORTRAIT OF ANTON ADRIAAN MUSSERT (PORTRET VAN ANTON ADRIAAN MUSSERT)

Production Company VPRO Television **Cinematography** Jaap Buis **Commentary** Hans Keller **Duration** 50 mins. B&W.

Books

Paul Verhoeven by Rob Van Scheers, Faber and Faber

Selected Interviews/Articles:

Best, no. 22 (new edition), 1998 (Starship Troopers)
Le Cinéphage, no. 5, 1992 (The Fourth Man)
Le Cinéphage, no. 14, 1994
Fog, no. 4, 1988 (RoboCop)
Première, no. 221, 1996 (Showgirls)
Première, no. 227, 1996 (Showgirls)
Starfix, no. 56, 1988 (RoboCop)
Starfix, no. 88, 1991 (Total Recall)

(all rights reserved):

Business is Business (© 1971 - Rob Houwer Films)
Turkish Delight (© 1973 - Rob Houwer Films)
Keetje Tippel (© 1975 - Rob Houwer Films)
Soldier of Orange (© 1977 - Rob Houwer Films/Gijs Versluys)
Spetters (© 1980 - Joop van den Ende)
The Fourth Man (© 1983 - United Film Company of the Netherlands)
Flesh + Blood (© 1985 - Riverside Pictures/Orion Pictures)
RoboCop (© 1987 - Orion Pictures)
Totall Recall (© 1990 - Carolco Pictures)
Basic Instinct (© 1992 - Carolco Pictures/Studio Canal +)
Showgirls (© 1995 - Carolco Pictures/Chargeurs)
Starship Troopers (© 1997 - Columbia Pictures-Tristar/Buena Vista Int.)
Hollow Man (© 2000 - Stephen Vaughan/SMPSP)
Hollow Man — special effects (page 64 © 2000 - Tippett Studio)

Unless otherwise stated all the other pictures are from
the archive of Paul Verhoeven.

Acknowledgments

This book would have never been possible
without the full co-operation of Paul Verhoeven.

I would like to thank the following persons:

Alan Marshall,
Alison Riback and Stacy Lumbrezer for their patience,
Chrissy Quesada for her help,
Lynn Ehrensperger,
Ed Neumeier for his insightful foreword
and my water-lily Anita.

And also:

Vincent Badia, Harry Bos, Tony Crawley, Walter Donohue and Richard Kelly,
Dominique Frotté, Frédéric Albert Lévy, Jeanne Seignourel, Gys Versluys.